Living in Ancient Greece

Titles in the Series Include:

Living in Ancient Egypt
Living in Ancient Rome
Living in Nazi Germany

Living in Ancient Greece

EXPLORING CULTURAL HISTORY

Don Nardo, *Book Editor*

Daniel Leone, *President*
Bonnie Szumski, *Publisher*
Scott Barbour, *Managing Editor*

GREENHAVEN
PRESS ®

THOMSON
★
™
GALE

San Diego • Detroit • New York • San Francisco • Cleveland
New Haven, Conn. • Waterville, Maine • London • Munich

THOMSON

GALE

© 2004 by Greenhaven Press. Greenhaven Press is an imprint of The Gale Group, Inc., a division of Thomson Learning, Inc.

Greenhaven® and Thomson Learning™ are trademarks used herein under license.

For more information, contact
Greenhaven Press
27500 Drake Rd.
Farmington Hills, MI 48331-3535
Or you can visit our Internet site at http://www.gale.com

ALL RIGHTS RESERVED.
No part of this work covered by the copyright hereon may be reproduced or used in any form or by any means—graphic, electronic, or mechanical, including photocopying, recording, taping, Web distribution or information storage retrieval systems—without the written permission of the publisher.

Every effort has been made to trace the owners of copyrighted material.

Cover credit: © Massimo Listri/CORBIS
Corel, 112
Dover Publications, 14
Library of Congress, 31
Photodisc, 105

LIBRARY OF CONGRESS CATALOGING-IN-PUBLICATION DATA

Living in ancient Greece / Don Nardo, book editor.
    p. cm. — (Exploring cultural history)
    Includes bibliographical references and index.
    ISBN 0-7377-1455-7 (pbk. : alk. paper) — ISBN 0-7377-1454-9 (lib. : alk. paper)
    1. Greece—Social life and customs. I. Nardo, Don, 1947– . II. Series.
DF78 .L49 2004
938—dc21
                                                                    2002192797

Printed in the United States of America

Contents

Foreword   8

Introduction: The Ancient Greeks—Founders of
Western Society   10

Chapter 1: People and Private Life

Chapter Preface   23

1. The Lives and Treatment of Slaves
   by Michael Grant   25
   An estimated one-third of Athens's population consisted of slaves during the Classical Age. Without slaves,
   most free men would have lacked the leisure time
   needed for pursuits like politics and philosophy.

2. Defining Wifely Duties
   by Xenophon   35
   The ancient Greek writer Xenophon penned a dialogue
   in which a country gentleman lists his wife's duties, as
   well as explains why men are intended to work outside
   the home and women within it.

3. Basic Forms of Classical Dress
   by Iris Brooke   42
   Almost all the clothing styles worn by the ancient
   Greeks were variations on a few basic, very simple
   forms, which could be wrapped, pleated, or decorated
   in more complex and distinctive ways.

4. Food and Dining
   by Andrew Dalby   47
   Whether they ate at home or dined out, Greeks across
   the Mediterranean sphere consumed a number of staple foods, among them wheat, barley, lentils, eggs,
   cheese, vegetables, fruits, and wine.

5. Education in Ancient Athens
   by Joint Association of Classical Teachers   53
   The majority of free Athenian boys went to private ele-
   mentary schools, where they learned to read and write.
   Some later went on to study at schools like Plato's
   Academy, which taught philosophy and science.

Chapter 2: Communal and Social Activities

Chapter Preface   60

1. How the World and Gods Came to Be
   by Hesiod   61
   The ancient Greek poet Hesiod described the creation myth in his *Theogony*. He tells how the heavens, earth, and gods came to be, including the tremendous battle for supremacy between the divine Titans and Olympians.

2. An Athenian on Trial for Murder
   by Lysias   70
   In this actual case of a Greek man on trial for killing his wife's lover, the accused hired a professional speechwriter to help put together a credible and persuasive defense.

3. The Athenian Assembly
   by Donald Kagan   78
   At the heart of Athens's unique collection of democratic institutions was the Assembly, in which citizens of all walks of life met and anyone could speak his mind and participate directly in government.

4. Banking and Local Industries
   by W.G. Hardy   84
   The large and prosperous Greek city-state of Athens featured a prominent artisan-merchant class that included, among others, potters, metalsmiths, jewelers, shoemakers, shopkeepers, bankers, and traders.

5. The Original Olympic Games
   by Judith Swaddling   91
   The most popular and prestigious of all the athletic competitions in the ancient world was the Olympic Games, held every four years at the Altis, Zeus's sacred sanctuary in southwestern Greece.

Chapter 3: Arts and Medicine

Chapter Preface   102

1. Constructing the Parthenon
   by Peter Green   103
   The most magnificent temple erected in ancient Greece

was the Parthenon, atop Athens's Acropolis. A virtual army of artists, craftspeople, and laborers toiled for nearly ten years to erect it.

2. Pottery Craftsmanship
   by Thomas Craven   110
   Pottery-making was a major industry in Greece, especially in Athens. There, potters produced vases and other vessels that achieved a perfect blend of practicality and beauty.

3. Increased Realism in Art, Literature, and Life
   by Michael Grant   116
   In Greece's Hellenistic Age (323–ca.30 B.C.), literature, sculpture, painting, and other artistic fields achieved more realism than in prior ages. Also, there was a new emphasis on the worth of the individual, which was reflected in better educational opportunities for both men and women.

4. Advances in Medical Science
   by Philip Wheelwright   125
   The renowned Greek physician Hippocrates and his followers advocated a revolutionary philosophic-scientific idea, namely that health and disease have natural, rather than supernatural, causes.

Chronology   130
For Further Research   134
Index   139
About the Editor   144

Foreword

Too often, history books and teachers place an overemphasis on events and dates. Students learn that key births, battles, revolutions, coronations, and assassinations occurred in certain years. But when many centuries separate these happenings from the modern world, they can seem distant, disconnected, even irrelevant.

The reality is that today's society is *not* disconnected from the societies that preceded it. In fact, modern culture is a sort of melting pot of various aspects of life in past cultures. Over the course of centuries and millennia, one culture passed on some of its traditions, in the form of customs, habits, ideas, and beliefs, to another, which modified and built on them to fit its own needs. That culture then passed on its own version of the traditions to later cultures, including today's. Pieces of everyday life in past cultures survive in our own lives, therefore. And it is often these morsels of tradition, these survivals of tried and true past experience, that people most cherish, take comfort in, and look to for guidance. As the great English scholar and archaeologist Sir Leonard Woolley put it, "We cannot divorce ourselves from our past. We are always conscious of precedents . . . and we let experience shape our views and actions."

Thus, for example, Americans and the inhabitants of a number of other modern nations can pride themselves on living by the rule of law, educating their children in formal schools, expressing themselves in literature and art, and following the moral precepts of various religions and philosophies. Yet modern society did not invent the laws, schools, literature, art, religions, and philosophies that pervade it; rather, it inherited these things from previous cultures. "Time, the great destroyer, is also the great preserver," the late, noted thinker Herbert J. Muller once observed. "It has preserved . . . the immense accumulation of products, skills, styles, customs, institutions, and ideas that make the man on the American street indebted to all the peoples of history, including some who never saw a street." In this way, ancient Mesopotamia gave the world its first cities and literature; ancient Egypt, large-scale architecture; ancient Israel, the formative concepts of Judaism,

Christianity, and Islam; ancient Greece, democracy, the theater, Olympic sports, and magnificent ceramics; ancient China, gunpowder and exotic fabrics; ancient Rome and medieval England, their pioneering legal systems; Renaissance Italy, great painting and sculpture; Elizabethan England, the birth of modern drama; and colonial America, the formative environments of the founders of the United States, the most powerful and prosperous nation in world history. Only by looking back on those peoples and how they lived can modern society understand its roots.

Not all the products of cultural history have been so constructive, however. Most ancient Greeks severely restricted the civil rights and daily lives of women, for instance; the Romans kept and abused large numbers of slaves, as did many Americans in the years preceding the Civil War; and Nazi Germany and the Soviet Union curbed or suppressed freedom of speech, assembly, and religion. Examining these negative aspects of life in various past cultures helps to expose the origins of many of the social problems that exist today; it also reminds us of the ever-present potential for people to make mistakes and pursue misguided or destructive social and economic policies.

The books in the Greenhaven Press Exploring Cultural History series provide readers with the major highlights of life in human cultures from ancient times to the present. The family, home life, food and drink, women's duties and rights, childhood and education, arts and leisure, literacy and literature, roads and means of communications, slavery, religious beliefs, and more are examined in essays grouped by theme. The essays in each volume have been chosen for their readability and edited to manageable lengths. Many are primary sources. These original voices from a past culture echo through the corridors of time and give the volume a strong feeling of immediacy and authenticity. The other essays are by historians and other modern scholars who specialize in the culture in question. An annotated table of contents, chronology, and extensive bibliography broken down by theme add clarity and context. Thus, each volume in the Greenhaven Press Exploring Cultural History series opens a unique window through which readers can gaze into a distant time and place and eavesdrop on life in a long vanished culture.

Introduction: The Ancient Greeks—Founders of Western Society

A ncient Greece has often been called the cradle of Western culture. Indeed, the Greeks, who called their land Hellas and themselves Hellenes, left behind a rich cultural heritage that constituted a key element in shaping later Western lands and peoples. Many of the social customs and habits and political concepts common in Europe and the United States today originated in ancient Greek society. At the same time, ancient Greek culture differed in many ways from its modern counterparts. And life in ancient Greece is all the more fascinating because it consisted of aspects both familiar and strange to modern eyes.

These aspects can be divided conveniently into two broad categories. The first consisted of life and culture on the larger communal level, which affected or benefited most or all members of society. Among these aspects were law and justice, large-scale religious worship, art and architecture, philosophy, theater and drama, and athletic competitions. Among the cultural aspects on a more personal level were the layout and furnishings of houses; the status, duties, and treatment of slaves, women, and children; and so forth. Sometimes these separate realms overlapped. Religious worship also took place on a small scale in the home, for instance; and the status of slaves and women determined which communal events they could attend. (Most women were barred from watching the events of the Olympic Games, and slaves often could not attend the theater.)

The Majestic Acropolis

Certainly everyone in the community benefited from the religious temples and other monumental stone structures built across the Greek world beginning in the sixth century B.C. These works, many of which are still partially intact, reached their height of magnificence during the following two centuries. Most famous of all was the huge and majestic complex of temples and other structures erected atop Athens's Acropolis (central hill) in the late fifth century B.C. (Athens was the largest and richest of the Greek city-states; most of the surviving evidence about ancient Greek life comes from Athens.)

These buildings were largely inspired by Pericles, an Athenian leader of extraordinary intelligence, vision, and imagination. His goal was to show that his city-state was the greatest in all Greece as well as to celebrate and honor the city's patron deity, Athena (goddess of wisdom and war). As the Greek biographer Plutarch wrote some five centuries later, this ambitious project was seen, both at the time and by posterity, as Pericles' and Athens's greatest cultural achievement:

> There was one measure above all which at once gave the greatest pleasure to the Athenians, adorned their city and created amazement among the rest of mankind, and which is today the sole testimony that the tales of the ancient power and glory of Greece are no mere fables. By this I mean his construction of temples and public buildings.[1]

Their communal religious function was not the only factor that tied these structures directly to the life of the community. They also required a wide variety of skills, as well as much backbreaking labor, to complete. And thousands of Athenians, free and slave, citizen and noncitizen, worked side by side on them. The most comprehensive description of the various kinds of workers involved is that from Plutarch's biography of Pericles, listing those who toiled to raise the largest and most beautiful temple in the complex—the Parthenon:

> The materials to be used were stone, bronze, ivory, gold, ebony, and cypress-wood, while the arts or trades which wrought or fashioned them were those of carpenter, modeler, coppersmith, stone-mason, dyer, worker in gold and ivory, painter, embroiderer, and engraver, and besides these the carriers and suppliers of the materials, such as merchants, sailors, and pilots for the seaborne traffic, and wagon-makers, trainers of draft-animals, and drivers for everything that came by land. There were also ropemakers, weavers, leatherworkers, road-builders, and miners. Each individual craft, like a general with an army under his separate command, had its own corps of unskilled laborers at its disposal . . . [and consequently] the city's prosperity was extended far and wide and shared among every age and condition in Athens.[2]

As anyone who has visited the Acropolis can attest, the workers' labors produced nothing less than spectacular results. Even in an advanced state of ruin, the Parthenon is an awesome sight that dominates the entire summit of the Acropolis. In its original state, the temple was 237 feet long, 110 feet wide, some 65 feet high, and incorporated over 22,000 tons of marble of exquisite quality. Inside stood a splendid 38-foot-high statue of Athena, with garments fashioned of beaten gold.

Sacrifice and Prayer

At various times of the year, the Acropolis temple complex, like similar (though smaller) ones in other Greek states, was the scene of large-scale public worship. Indeed, unlike the situation in most modern societies, in which religion is viewed as a private affair, the Greeks saw it as a public concern. They felt that it was vital to a community's welfare to maintain the goodwill of the gods. And impiety—lacking faith in or respect for the gods—was a serious offense, for if one person offended the gods, the deities might bring down their wrath on the whole community.

During the larger religious festivals celebrated by all members of a Greek city-state, the participants performed the principle element of Greek worship—sacrifice. Conforming to ancient traditions, Greek animal sacrifice consisted of set rituals. First, the worshipers draped flower garlands over the animal, referred to as the victim, as they led it to the altar. (Altars were always set up outdoors. No worship took place inside a temple out of respect for the god's privacy.) Next, a priest or priestess poured water over the altar to purify it and sprinkled barley grains on the victim for the same purpose. Then he or she used a club to stun the animal and a knife to cut its throat, drained the blood into a bowl, and sprinkled some of it on the altar (or over the worshipers). Finally, several priests used axes and knives to slaughter the victim. The bones and organs were wrapped in the fat and burned, generating smoke that, it was believed, rose up to nourish and appease the gods; meanwhile the worshipers divided, cooked, and ate the meat.

Prayer was another pillar of Greek worship, performed during almost every life ritual, from meals and marriages to funerals and travel departures. A Greek prayed standing, with his or her hands raised, palm upwards. If the god being addressed dwelled beneath the earth, the worshiper might stretch his or her arms downward or stomp on the ground to get the god's attention. To kneel or bow in prayer, a common modern custom, was seen as unworthy of a free person. Also, prayers were usually said aloud unless the worshiper had some special reason to conceal them.

Any Greek could pray or perform sacrifice on his or her own, so there were no priests in the modern sense of full-time spiritual guides. When family members prayed together at their home altars, the head of the household led the ritual; in larger public ceremonies, a clan or tribal leader or a leading state official usually took charge. In addition, various temples and cults (religious congregations) often had part- or full-time staffs of caretakers and specially trained individuals who initiated or aided in sacrifices and other rituals. Any of the people just described might bear the title of priest or priestess.

The Birth of Philosophy and Science

Though nearly all Greeks were devoutly religious, Greek thinkers, known as philosophers (a term taken from Greek words meaning "love of wisdom"), did not shy away from looking for meaning in nature beyond the realm and actions of the gods. This was partly because the gods were seen as vastly more powerful versions of people, coexisting within nature alongside humans, rather than as perfect beings who created nature. Thus, when Greek philosophers began searching for the underlying principles of nature, they largely removed the gods and other supernatural elements from the discussion. As modern scientists do, they tended to see the heavenly bodies and other facets of nature as material objects obeying natural laws rather than as personalized beings.

Beginning in the sixth century B.C., a few generations of Greek philosophers inquired into diverse aspects of nature. And in so doing they laid the foundation for most of the major scientific disciplines, including astronomy, physics, chemistry, biology, and medicine. The wide range of ideas and information stimulated by their inquiry filtered down to many on the Greek street. It was not unusual to see groups of people, both literate and illiterate, listening to lectures or engaging in intellectual discussions in public places. The inquiry of philosophers also inspired the establishment of schools of higher learning (academies), such as those founded by Plato and Aristotle in Athens. Over time, tens of thousands of young men from all corners of the Greek world attended these schools.

The Greek thinkers who attempted to penetrate the secrets of nature and the cosmos included, among many others, Thales of Miletus (flourished circa 600), who concluded that nature's underlying physical principle was water; Anaximander (ca. 611–547 B.C.), who disagreed, saying instead that the universal principle was a less tangible substance, which he called "the Boundless"; Pythagoras (sixth century B.C.), who saw mathematical complexity as a basic natural principle; and Democritus (ca. 460– ca. 357), who developed an early version of the atomic theory, suggesting that all matter is composed of tiny, invisible particles called atoms. Modern scholars label all of these thinkers "pre-Socratic" because they predated the Athenian philosopher Socrates.

Italian artist Raphael's the School of Athens *portrays many notable ancient Greek thinkers.*

The life and teachings of Socrates marked an important turning point, namely the beginning of a major separation between Greek philosophy and science. He opposed studying nature, saying that to concentrate on the physical, mechanical aspects of things would divert one's attention from what was really important. This, he said, was an understanding of the meaning of such ethical concepts as goodness, wisdom, and justice, and how human beings should best apply them to improve themselves and society. Socrates, who left no writings of his own, made a profound impression on two of his followers, Plato and Xenophon. Xenophon later said of Socrates,

> [He was] so devout that he never did anything without the sanction of the gods, so upright that he never did the slightest harm to anybody . . . so wise that he never made a mistake in deciding between better and worse. . . . He seemed to me to be the perfect example of goodness and happiness.[3]

Also deeply concerned with ethical concepts and the human condition were Plato (427–347 B.C.) and later his student, Aristotle (384–322 B.C.). In his dialogue *Meno*, for example, Plato explores the question, "Can virtue be taught?" However, these two literary and philosophical giants did not confine themselves strictly to ethics, as Socrates had done. They each turned out a vast array of works covering a wide range of subjects, from politics to literary criticism. They also carried on important scientific research or speculation. Plato's *Timaeus*, for instance, deals with the formation of the universe; and Aristotle made huge strides in the fields of biology and zoology, including an ingenious system for classifying animals.

Drama and Theater

The Greeks developed other branches of creative thinking and writing besides philosophy. Among the more important, especially in its profound effects on later ages, including the present one, was drama. Beginning in the early fifth century B.C., a small group of Athenian playwrights created Western drama and established its major themes, conventions, and tone. The leading playwrights of that era, who are still viewed among the giants of the genre, were the tragedians Aeschylus, Sophocles, and Euripides, and the comic genius Aristophanes.

At the same time, the Athenians invented a specialized venue in which to perform the plays these men wrote—the theater. The earliest version of their Theater of Dionysus (the fertility god to whom the theatrical presentations were dedicated) was constructed during the early 490s B.C. By the mid-fifth century B.C., it consisted of a circular "dancing place"—the orchestra—where the actors performed; entrances for the performers on two sides of the orchestra; an audience area (the *theatron,* source of the word *theater*) with wooden (later stone) bleachers accommodating a maximum of some fourteen thousand people; and a "scene building" (the *skene,* source of the word *scene*). Located in front of and facing the orchestra and *theatron,* the scene building served as a background for the performers and probably contained dressing rooms and storage spaces for stage props.

Usually, a play began when the actors and chorus, accompanied by one or more musicians, marched into the orchestra singing an entrance song. They kept in strict formation, moving and gesturing in unison. Once the story began to unfold, the chorus members broke formation, moved from place to place, and reacted to the play's characters and events with appropriate verses and gestures. Among the chorus's several possible functions were to ask the characters probing questions and give them advice (both of which illuminated the story's themes); and to set the play's overall mood by the tone of its singing and reciting.

The actors who engaged in interplay with the chorus wore elaborate masks, usually made of linen stiffened with clay and brightly painted. "The masks worn by the chorus and actors seem to have been fairly standardized," comments noted scholar Bernard M.W. Knox.

> There were recognizable types—old man, middle-aged man, youth, old woman, etc. . . . The masks certainly ruled out the play of facial expression which we regard today as one of the actor's most important skills, but in the Theater of Dionysus, where even the front row of spectators was sixty feet away from the stage . . . facial expression could not have been seen anyway. And the masks had a practical value. They made it possible for the same actor to play two or even three or four different parts in different scenes of the play.[4]

Masks also made it possible for men to play women's parts, an important and closely observed theatrical convention. The Athenians, like most other Greeks, considered it improper for women to bare their emotions, even staged ones, in public.

The actors also wore brightly colored costumes. This was partly to catch the eye from a distance since most of the spectators sat so far from the actors. In addition, the colors aided in character recognition; for example, a queen's gown would be purple, the traditional color of royalty in ancient times. The actors used props, too, as they do today, although the Greeks used them more sparingly. The most common props were chariots, couches, statues of gods, shields and swords, and biers to display dead bodies.

The plays presented in the Theater of Dionysus were highly entertaining and widely popular. The proof is that during the fifth century B.C. its performances were always sold out. Because the number of people who desired entrance far exceeded the facility's seating capacity, it was necessary for the Athenians to introduce still another innovation that has survived to the present—the theater ticket. The tickets took the form of tokens resembling coins and were made of bronze, lead, ivory, bone, or terra-cotta.

Athenian vs. Spartan Women

Visible in the audience during a play presented in Athens were persons from all social classes and walks of life (except slaves, who were usually, though not necessarily always, excluded). Many of these same people met in other public gatherings, the most important being those connected with the city's democracy, the world's first (established in 508 B.C.). All free adult Athenian citizens, except women, could vote to choose their leaders and pass or reject new laws. In time, a number of other Greek states adopted democratic systems similar to that of Athens.

However, the fact that women could not vote or hold public office shows that, for all its virtues, Athenian democracy had a serious flaw. Namely, it did not recognize that all people in society possessed innate dignity and deserved equal opportunity under the law. Slavery was an entrenched institution, for instance. Slaves had no legal rights or say in deciding their own destinies, and some suffered serious abuse or even death at the hands of their masters (although most household slaves were generally well treated). At least Athenian women were considered citizens with some rights. They were designated *astai*, meaning "citizens without political rights." An *aste* had the civic rights to take part in and/or benefit from the community's religious and economic institutions. Thus, for example, women played roles, often im-

Ancient Greece

Greek lands

portant ones, in various religious festivals.

However, it would be a mistake to generalize about the lives of all Greek women based solely on evidence from Athens. Although Athenian women were, for the most part, dominated by men, forced to spend most of their time in the home, led highly restricted lives, and were not allowed to own land, not all Greek women were in the same position. The most prominent exception was the case of Spartan women. (Sparta, located in the Peloponnesus, the large peninsula making up the southern third of Greece, was a militaristic state and Athens's chief rival.) Spartan women engaged in vigorous physical training similar to (but not as intense as) that of Spartan men and were certainly capable of fighting if the need so arose.

Spartan women also enjoyed numerous rights and privileges that many other Greek women did not. First, it appears that women in Sparta did not simply manage the household for their husbands, as women in Athens did, but actually set the rules and largely took precedence over men in that sphere. This was because Spartan society was long built around a strict, regimented system designed to produce machinelike soldiers to man the most feared army in Greece. Spartan boys left home at age seven, and up to the age of thirty or more they lived in military barracks with other males. In fact, Spartan men were not allowed to reside with their wives and children until age thirty. And even then, married men were frequently absent, engaging in military training, war, hunting, and political activities.

The domestic power of Spartan women manifested itself in a number of ways. They were not largely confined to the home and could be quite outspoken and assertive, often standing up, without fear, to their husbands, sons, and other men. Plutarch compiled a large collection of anecdotes about Spartan women. In one, the daughter of a Spartan king boldly interrupts his negotiations with a foreign ambassador, saying, "Father, this miserable little foreigner will ruin you completely unless you drive him out of the house pretty quickly." Another Spartan woman, Plutarch says, "After hearing that her son was a coward and unworthy of her . . . killed him when he made his appearance."[5] Such incidents would have been unthinkable in Athens and in many other parts of Greece.

Spartan women could even own land. Although Spartan inheritance laws remain unclear, apparently a daughter could inherit a share of her father's land even when she had brothers, her share being half that of a male. And if she had no natural or adopted brother, she likely inherited the family property directly, without the obligation of marrying a male relative, as was the case in Athens. As a result, a good deal of land eventually fell into the hands of Spartan women. Aristotle, who complained in his *Politics* that female Spartans had entirely too much freedom, reported that in his day they owned fully two-fifths of the land in Sparta.

Children's Lives

Whatever rights they may have enjoyed, Spartan women shared one fundamental, essential duty with Greek women everywhere. They were expected to produce children to perpetuate the family, the most basic and traditional social unit. Unfortunately, Greek child-rearing customs reflected a general view of children that most people today would view as misguided and counter to the development of healthy self-esteem. In general, childhood was not viewed as an enviable, happy time of life, as it often is today. And adults felt little or no nostalgia for their youth. This was partly because they believed that children lacked proper reasoning powers, courage, or even a moral capacity until they were at least in their teens. The common wisdom was that young children needed to be closely watched, carefully trained, and, when necessary, harshly disciplined by parents, tutors, and other community members.

This does not mean that Greek children led joyless lives. To the contrary, they played, often with toys familiar to modern children, such as balls, hoops, tops, dolls (made of wood, clay, or rags) and dollhouses (complete with furniture), yo-yos, and miniature carts and chariots.

However, the most important pastime of childhood (for males, at least) was education. Young girls were trained at home by their mothers in weaving and other household arts, although some vase paintings suggest that at least a few girls learned to read. In Athens during Pericles' and Socrates' time, boys aged seven began attending private schools in which they learned reading and writing and eventually the verses of Homer and other poets. Boys also learned singing, playing the lyre (harp), and physical education (athletic events and dancing).

By the late fifth century B.C., higher education in Athens could be obtained for a fee from roving teachers called sophists. They raised the ire of traditionalists, who disapproved of their use of rhetoric (the art of persuasive speaking) to make both sides in an argument seem equally valid. Beginning in the century that followed, some young men also studied at the academies, such as Plato's Academy and Aristotle's Lyceum.

On the whole, education in many other Greek poleis was presumably similar to that in Athens. Perhaps not surprisingly, the major exception appears to have been Sparta. There, the education of boys and young men was, like most other social institutions, built around the needs and aims of the military establishment. First, Spartan elders examined all male infants. And those considered too weak were exposed (left outside to die). Those who made it past this initial test faced years of relentless state-sponsored schooling and training, which emphasized the boy's ability to endure hardships and become a strong, fearsome soldier. (There was some instruction in dancing, patriotic songs, and poetry, but these subjects took a decided backseat to military training.)

Spartan girls also received an education at state expense, the only women in all of Greece known to have enjoyed this privilege. The nature of this learning is unclear but seems to have emphasized physical fitness (probably to help facilitate having many baby boys to replenish the army ranks). Some girls may also have learned reading and other skills. Thus, the nature and quality of life in ancient Greece could vary widely, depending on factors such as where one lived, one's gender, and whether one was free or a slave.

Notes

1. Plutarch, *Life of Pericles*, in *The Rise and Fall of Athens: Nine Greek Lives by Plutarch*, trans. Ian Scott-Kilvert. New York: Penguin, 1960, p. 177.

2. Plutarch, *Pericles*, in *Rise and Fall of Athens*, pp. 178–79.

3. Xenophon, *Memoirs*, in *Xenophon: Conversations with Socrates*, trans. Hugh Tredennick and Robin Waterfield. New York: Penguin, 1990, p. 216.

4. Bernard M.W. Knox, trans., *Oedipus the King*. New York: Pocket Books, 1959, pp. xxii–xxiii.

5. Plutarch, *Sayings of Spartan Women*, *Plutarch on Sparta*, trans. Richard J.A. Talbert. New York: Penguin, 1988, pp. 158–59.

People and Private Life

CHAPTER

1

Chapter Preface

Looking back on the twentieth century, most aspects of private life in industrialized countries like the United States have undergone constant and significant change. Styles of clothes, houses, and furniture, as well as the kinds of foods consumed, composition of family units, roles and duties of women in the family, schools and education, and so forth are today all drastically different than they were in the year 1900. By contrast, private life in Athens and other ancient Greek cities was steeped in and guided by centuries of tradition; and very little changed from one generation to another. For example, dress styles at the beginning of the Classical Age, about 500 B.C., were hardly any different when that period ended more than a century and a half later. And virtually no attempts were made in that or succeeding ancient eras to alter or alleviate the institution of slavery and the customs surrounding it.

Slavery was certainly one of the major facets of private life in Greek society. Most households, with the exception of the poorest, had at least one slave. Wealthy families had as many as ten or more slaves. Not only did many free Greeks come to rely on slaves to do most of the menial chores, but Greek men with slaves had more free time for more edifying and pleasurable pursuits, including politics, philosophy, and athletics.

Another cornerstone of the average Greek household consisted of the contributions made by its women. The duties, social status, and treatment of women varied from one Greek city-state or region to another. However, with a few exceptions (such as in the militaristic state of Sparta), Greek women led restricted, sheltered lives. They could not take part in politics, and they were expected to do the bidding of their husbands and other male relatives. Still, women were highly industrious and performed tasks crucial to both private life and the community in general, including having and rearing children, supervising the household (including its slaves), making clothes, and even paying the bills. Along with the household slaves, wives, mothers, and daughters also prepared the meals, which featured a wide variety of nutritious and tasty foods.

Women played a much smaller role in another aspect of private life—education. Of the students who attended a community's privately run elementary classes (which usually met in the back room of a shop), almost all were young men. Young women were generally tutored at home by one or both parents. After receiving instruction in literature, music, and athletics, some young men went on to higher education in academies such as those established in Athens by the noted philosophers Plato and Aristotle.

The Lives and Treatment of Slaves

Michael Grant

This effective summary of the institution of slavery as it was practiced in ancient Greece is by the distinguished classical historian Michael Grant. Drawing on a wide array of ancient Greek writers, from Homer and Hesiod to Xenophon, Plato, and Aristotle, Grant discusses the numbers of Greek slaves, how they came to be slaves, their status, varying treatment, duties and professions, and the ways that philosophers and other writers rationalized and justified the institution.

S lavery seems an appallingly inhumane institution, because its essential feature is that slaves have no independence or rights or legal personalities of their own, but are the property of their masters. Slavery was a feature of every advanced ancient civilization, not only those of the Greeks and Romans. And those Greeks and Romans who played a large part in public life or made important contributions to literature and art were enabled to do so by means of the spare time, or leisure, and financial surpluses, conferred upon them by their slaves (this was the only way in which such a surplus could be acquired).

There were various forms and nuances of ancient labour. . . . But it was slavery, chattel slavery, that was the most significant kind of unfree labour at the highest periods of Greek and Roman history. Even if never . . . predominant, it was extensive and general, and inherent in the very conception of the ancient state. Every action, belief or institution was in some way or other affected by the possibility that someone involved might be a slave. The contribution of slave labour was essential, so that it is justifiable to describe Greece and Rome as, to a large extent, slave societies, such as do not exist today, at least in the western world.

To insist on the history of the 'rights' of slaves is not very rel-

Michael Grant, *A Social History of Greece and Rome*. New York: Scribner's, 1992. Copyright © 1992 by Michael Grant Publications, Ltd. Reproduced by permission of the publisher.

evant. For, basically, they had none. Their total contrast with free men was a familiar rhetorical point. They were even regarded as kinless, and in Greece their marriages were unrecognised, and their owners could prevent them from taking place. The exploitation of slaves was based upon the direct use, or sanction, of force, not upon the 'free' play of economy, as in capitalist societies. This was the most extreme way in which one social group could use its power for economic advantage. Plato noted that the protection and defence of slave-holders was a crucial function of the government, and Aristotle described the master-slave relationship as one of three most basic features of the household— slaves being the best, most manageable, and most necessary property a man could possess. A slave was not expected to display virtues, and the comic dramatist Menander gave his slaves special masks, displaying mental disharmony and moral deviance, to be expected from men who were mostly non-Greeks, and therefore natural barbarians and enemies. Their treatment, of course, varied. Relying on their lack of rights, a master might vilify or beat them with immunity. Or, remembering their indispensable services, he might choose to treat them decently— within the limits of their status. The result might be warm mutual affection. . . .

Or, alternatively, relations between master and slave might be deplorable.

Slaves' Numbers and Status

What percentage of the total population of the Greek *poleis* the slaves constituted has been much debated and argued; and, in any case, each state was constituted differently. One recent estimate suggests that in the classical Athens of the fifth and fourth centuries there were between 80,000 and 100,000 slaves of both sexes, representing about one-third of the total population. But some say there were more, and some less. Anyway there were a lot, and there was always a sufficient supply of them. A very large number of these slaves were foreigners—there was a general opinion that one ought not to have Greek slaves—and they were obtained by capture in war, by sale in the huge slave-markets such as Delos (of which we know too little), and by birth to those who were already slavewomen.

How far all this slavery kept down the pay of free workers—who shared so many occupations with them—remains uncertain, but it must surely have done so (although we can detect no protests from the free poor) and must have caused some contempt for free labour. Numerous slaves worked in the basic field of agriculture, but many others in industry and public works. And another disputed question is the extent to which slavery impeded technological improvement, and so industrial advance. Once again, it must surely to some extent have done so—because when so much slave labour was at hand, even if not wholly efficient, why bother about better technology or rationalisation of production methods?

However, the slaves, although numerous, did not do *most* of Greek production. And the work they did was often in their master's household, to satisfy his needs and those of his family. Others could be hired out to a third party, or allowed to work independently, for instance as craftsmen. Others, again, had the state, not an individual, as their master. Some of these worked in mines, for instance Athens's notorious silver-mines in Laurium. That is to say they, and their functions, were varied and flexible, so that efforts to describe them as a single social 'class' must be rejected.

Slaves were at first not very numerous in Greece, but they always existed. Homeric slaves, being the products of wars and raids and piracy, were mostly women, but not all: Eumaeus, in the *Odyssey*, had been sold into slavery, and there were other male slaves as well. The households of Alcinous and Odysseus were said to possess fifty slaves each, but that is a conventional figure. In spite of the very low estimate accorded to impoverished free men, 'Zeus', remarks Eumaeus, 'takes away half a man's worth when the day of slavery comes upon him.'

Yet [the eighth-century B.C. Greek farmer and poet] Hesiod represented a widespread view when he saw slavery as essential to his slave-owning class. Another early writer, Aesop, was a slave himself, from Thrace, which was where so many slaves came from. He is a partly legendary figure, but seems to have written the earliest collection of fables. Whether he expressed views about the disadvantages of the slave status, or employed the slave situation to universalise the human experience, must remain conjectural.

In archaic Greece, slavery was still not very extensive. But then, in the sixth century, there was an astronomical increase. This was partly because Solon, at the beginning of the sixth cen-

---

A Greek Claims Slavery Is Natural

The Greek philosopher and scientist Aristotle (384–322 B.C.) composed his Politics *in the late 340s B.C., in which, among other things, he asserts that slavery is a natural state of affairs. In retrospect, his logic in justifying slavery is faulty because it is based mainly on the simple observation of existing circumstances rather than on moral and ethical concerns.*

Also, as regards male and female, the former is superior, the latter inferior; the male is ruler, the female is subject. It must also be that the same is true for the whole of mankind. Where there is a difference between people, like that between soul and body, or between man and mere animal (this being the condition of people whose function is to use their bodies, manual labor being the best service they can give, for such people are by nature slaves), it is better for the lower ones to be ruled, just as it is for the subjects mentioned above. A man is a slave by nature if he *can* belong to someone else (this is why he does in fact belong to someone else) or if he has reason to the extent of understanding it without actually possessing it. Animals other than man do not obey reason, but follow their instincts. There is only a slight difference between the services rendered by slaves and by animals: both give assistance with their bodies for the attainment of the essentials of living.

Nature tries to make a difference between slave and free, even as to their bodies—making the former strong, with a view to their doing the basic jobs, and making the free people upright, useless for servile jobs but suitable for political life, which is divided into the tasks of war and of peace. The opposite, however, often turns out to be the case: it happens that some have the physique of free men, whereas others have the souls. It is quite obvious that if people showed their differences in their mere physique, as the statues of the gods show the difference between gods and men, everyone would say that the inferior ones ought to be slaves of the others.

If this is true of the body, it is even more just for the distinction to apply to the soul. But it is not so easy to see the beauty of the soul as the beauty of the body. It is clear, then, that people are by nature free men or slaves, and that it is expedient and just for those who are slaves to be ruled.

Aristotle, *Politics*, trans. A.E. Wardman in Renford Bambrough, ed., *The Philosophy of Aristotle*. New York: New American Library, 1963, pp. 388–89.

tury, abolished debt-bondage at Athens (though at other cities it remained in force). . . . It meant that Athens, deprived of the forced labour of its serfs, had to import many additional slaves from elsewhere to take the place of those who had thus been released from their serf-like obligations.

When wars broke out, slaves got new chances. For one thing, a city-state's mobilisation of free urban troops for war depended on the maintenance of production by the slaves who remained at home. And, furthermore, the slaves themselves were sometimes enrolled to fight. This occurred during internal convulsions (*staseis*), but it was also not unknown in external wars. Whether slaves fought against the Persians at Salamis is uncertain, but certainly they rowed in the Peloponnesian War, notably at Arginusae (406), though this was recognised as exceptional; and they occasionally served as soldiers as well.

They also made their mark in civilian capacities too. For example, some of the leading potters and vase-painters were almost certainly slaves. And in the labour force on the Acropolis slaves worked alongside free men. Increasing democracy at Athens, and emphasis on the rights of poor citizens, enhanced the general reliance on slavery. That is to say, individual freedom flourished when slavery was abundant as well. At Athens there were large private workshops manned by slaves, such as those of Lysias and his brother, and Pasion—both factories for making shields. But there were also other new, upwardly mobile, opportunities for slaves (still within their slave status), although always, of course, the iron distinction which kept them apart from, and under, free men was maintained.

Why, given this new degree of possible latitude, did the slaves in classical Athens not revolt? Partly because, being foreigners from all parts, they were polyglot and multi-ethnic, possessing no degree of unity. But what they did, instead, was to run away, and fugitive slaves were always a major problem; they could count on some degree of religious asylum. During the Peloponnesian War, after the Spartans fortified Deceleia in Attica, a very large number of the slaves employed by the Athenians at their Laurium silver-mines defected to the other side.

In the following century, Athenian slave-owners displayed a tendency to replace enforced obedience by attempting to encourage spontaneous obedience, so that the legal personality of slaves began to emerge. True, people were still frightened of them, and were still eager enough to equate them with barbarians—enemies, against whose threat military training was necessary—and the 'free poor' struggled to maintain the citizen-slave distinction. Yet Athenian law came to protect slaves, in a limited way, and their killing was prohibited. Such sanctions, however, were religious or social rather than legal; and constraints on slave-masters were not so much motivated by a desire to protect the slaves as by the wish to protect the state against over-powerful slave-masters.

Attempts to Rationalize Slavery

During the fifth and fourth centuries the writers all had their say on this theme. Herodotus, while denouncing the corporate en-slavement of Greek states to the Persians, accepted *individual* slavery as the will of the gods. Euripides, as always, was more critical, observing that a good slave could have 'internal' free-dom, and be a better person than a free man. He was echoing the sophists' (minority) view that slavery was *not* natural—so that it could not degrade anyone who was not 'really' a slave. A slave, that is to say, could be 'free in mind'. As Euripides causes a mes-senger, himself of slave status, to remark:

> It's low not to feel with your masters,
> Laugh with them, and sympathise in their sorrows.
> Born to service as I am, I would be
> Numbered among the noble
> Slaves, unfree in name,
> Free in mind. Better this than for one man
> To be doubly cursed—a slave in mind
> As well as slave in the words of his fellows.   [*Helen* 726–733]

The comic dramatist Aristophanes, however, although he boasted of abandoning conventional jokes about slaves, did not really accept them as human beings. His conservative contem-porary, known as the Old Oligarch, believed that in Athens they were too well treated!

Unrestraint on the part of slaves and resident aliens is very prevalent with the Athenians, and it isn't permitted to beat them there, nor will a slave stand aside for you.

I'll explain what's behind the local practice: if it were lawful for a free person to beat a slave, resident alien, or freedman, lots of Athenians mistaken for slaves would get beaten. For the populace there is no better in its clothing than slaves and resident aliens, and its appearance is no better. If someone is amazed at this too, that they let slaves live it up and in some cases to lead lives of great splendour: this too they would seem to do on considered opinion. For where there is naval power it is necessary for slaves to work for money . . . And where there are rich slaves there is no longer any advantage in my slave's being afraid of you.

Xenophon, aware of what the sophists had said, declared that

The painting on this ancient vase shows slaves working in a shop, tended by their overseer (at far right).

the 'real' slave is the bad (free) man, in bondage to his own faults and lusts, whereas whether one is, or is not, an actual slave, is an accident of fortune—a convenient sop to the consciences of slave-owners: who, he also, more ominously, suggested, ought to avail themselves of unpaid bodyguards against the danger that slaves presented.

Something has already been said about Plato's and Aristotle's views on the subject; but it may be added that Plato felt an aristocratic contempt for slaves, as well as for other manual workers, and barbarians. He saw no theoretical justification for the view that slavery was a mere convention, and his *Laws* are severer on slaves than the actual laws of his time.

Aristotle, however, provides the only surviving ancient attempt at a determined analysis of slavery. Like Plato, he considered it perfectly right and proper that some people are slaves. Aware of men who held the opposite view, he disagreed with them, maintaining that barbarians, for example, are slaves by nature, and that men conquered in war legitimately became the property of the ruler: the rule of the free man over the slave is a necessary institution:

> The slave is not merely the slave of the master but wholly belongs to the master. These considerations therefore make clear the nature of the slave and his essential quality: one who is a human being belonging by nature not to himself but to another is by nature a slave . . .

After a prolonged and intricate argument Aristotle comes down firmly in favour of the principle of natural slavery: 'there exist certain persons who are essentially slaves everywhere, and certain others who are so nowhere . . . it is just and proper for the one party to be governed and the other to govern by the form of government for which they are by nature fitted'.

The author of the *Oeconomica*, which was preserved under the name of Aristotle [but written by an unknown author, usually called the Pseudo-Aristotle], reflected upon the character of a slave's existence:

> The slave who is best suited for his work is the kind that is neither too cowardly nor too courageous . . .

> Three things make up the life of a slave, work, punishment and

food. To give them food but no punishment and no work makes them insolent. And that they should have work and punishment but no food is tyrannical and destroys their efficiency. It remains therefore to give them work and sufficient food; for it is impossible to rule over slaves without offering rewards, and a slave's reward is food . . . and since the drinking of wine makes even free men insolent . . . it is clear that wine ought never to be given to slaves, or at any rate very seldom.

Meanwhile, however, the politician Hyperides proposed that slaves should be granted citizenship in order to fight against King Philip II of Macedonia. As for [the Greek playwright] Menander (342/1–293/89 BC), he is aware of the literary and comic tradition, from the slave-owner's point of view, that slaves are lazy, sex-crazed or gluttonous, and need to be beaten. But some of his slaves (who figure extensively in his plays) are also clever and resourceful schemers—useful to free men, and helping them to see themselves as they are. As for the supply of slaves, he took it for granted that piracy would remain one of the principal sources. . . .

Hellenistic Greece did not add a great deal. The slave-markets were active, because of wars and continued kidnapping by pirates, though slavery was also perpetuated by breeding. The Seleucid monarch Antiochus IV Epiphanes possessed a huge number of slaves of his own, and we hear (from a later age it is true) that they constituted one-third of the population of Pergamum. At Chios, in the third century BC, there was a slave rebellion under a certain Drimacus (this was another place where slaves were particularly abundant). In Ptolemaic Egypt the picture is mixed. There were not, it appears, a great many chattel slaves, since the free poor took their place. But we hear not only of debt-bondage but of various kinds of domestic slaves—and even of female slaves owned by women—and in the second century BC there was an Egyptian school for slaves.

In general, the idea of 'rights' for slaves began to take shape gradually, prompted by the growing individualism of the Hellenistic age. Attitudes varied, and the views of the Stoics were not altogether illiberal. True, they were somewhat contemptuous of slaves, but they did feel that the whole institution needed to be defined, and, in particular, that slaves ought to be properly treated. For slaves were allowed a capacity for virtue, seeing that moral status, the Stoics pointed out, depended on the soul, so that social status was irrelevant—and very often due to capricious fortune: the wise man alone is free, and the bad man is a slave. The actual state of slavery, that is to say, as many people felt at the time, was 'an accident': unnatural perhaps, but indispensable and a fact of life.

Defining Wifely Duties

Xenophon

The noted Athenian general and historian Xenophon (ZEN-uh-phon) composed his *Oeconomicus* sometime in the mid-fourth century B.C. while he was living on his estate at Scillus, near Olympia. Translated variously as *The Householder* and *The Estate Manager*, the work purports to demonstrate the efficient way to run a country estate. As Plato frequently did, Xenophon chose as a format a dialogue between two characters, one of them the martyred philosopher Socrates, whom Xenophon had known well. Although the other speaker is a country gentleman named Ischomachus, that character is clearly a thinly disguised representation of Xenophon himself. One of the most fascinating and engaging sections of the work concerns Ischomachus's young wife, who, through his recollections, contributes some dialogue of her own. Their conversation reveals her age when they wed (fourteen) and much information about the expectations the husband has for her and their long-term relationship. Ischomachus/Xenophon sees it as his happy duty to teach his wife about life and views marriage as a partnership ordained by the gods. He also provides a rationale for making a woman the overseer of the home and a detailed list of the duties she is expected to perform.

"I'd be very grateful if you could tell me something," I said. "When you're not engaged like this, where do you spend your time, and what do you do? You see, I want very much to find out from you what activities have gained you the reputation of being truly good. For, as I can also tell from looking at your physical condition, you don't spend time indoors."

'Ischomachus smiled at my question as to what he did to have gained the reputation of being truly good (I got the impression that he was pleased), and said, "I don't know whether people call me that when they're talking to you about me. When I am summoned to an exchange of property, where the issue is financing

Xenophon, "The Estate-Manager," *Conversations of Socrates*, translated by Hugh Tredennick and Robin Waterfield. New York: Penguin Books, 1990. Copyright © 1990 by Robin Waterfield. Reproduced by permission of the publisher.

a trireme or a chorus, no one goes looking for 'Truly Good' but the summons calls me plain 'Ischomachus', the name my father gave me! Anyway, Socrates," he went on, "to answer your question, I don't spend any time at all indoors: my wife is perfectly capable of managing my household affairs by herself."

'"I've got a question on this too, Ischomachus," I said. "I'd be very glad if you could tell me whether you personally taught your wife how to be a model wife, or whether, when you were given her by her parents, she already knew how to manage her sphere or responsibility."

'"How on earth could she know that when I received her, Socrates?" he asked. "She wasn't yet fifteen years old when she came to me, and in her life up till then considerable care had been taken that she should see and hear and discover as little as possible. Don't you think one should be content if all she knew when she came was how to turn wool into a cloak, and all she'd seen was how wool-spinning is assigned to the female servants? I was content, Socrates," he added, "because when she came, she'd been excellently coached as far as her appetite was concerned, and that seems to me to be the most important training, for the husband as well as the wife."

Marriage Is a Partnership

'"What about all the other things she needed to know, Ischomachus?" I asked. "Did you personally teach your wife how to be capable of looking after them?"

'"Well, at any rate not, you can be sure, until I had made a sacrifice to the gods," said Ischomachus, "and had prayed that I would teach and she would learn what was best for both of us."

'"And did your wife join in your sacrificing, and offer up the same prayers?" I asked.

'"She certainly did," said Ischomachus. "She made many vows to the gods, and prayed that she might become a model wife. It was obvious that she would be a responsible pupil."

'"Please tell me where you started, Ischomachus," I said. "What did you teach her first? I'd rather hear you describe this than the most spectacular athletic competition or horse-race!"

'"All right, Socrates," said Ischomachus in reply. "I waited until she'd been broken in and was tame enough for a conversation,

and then I asked her something along the following lines: 'Tell
me, my dear: have you realized yet why I married you and why
your parents gave you to me? I mean, I know, and it's clear to
you too, that it wouldn't have been difficult for each of us to have
found someone else to share our beds. But for my part, I was
considering whom it was in my interest to get as the best person
to share my home and my children, and your parents had your
interests at heart; so I chose you, and your parents apparently
preferred me to all other eligible candidates. Now, as far as children are concerned, we will wait to see if God grants us and before thinking about how best to bring them up: one of the ad-
vantages we will share with each other is having them to support
us and look after us as well as they can when we grow old. But
what we share now is this home of ours, and we share it because
I make all my income available for both of us, and you have de-
posited all that you brought with you in the same common pool.
There's no need to tot up which of us has made the greater contribution quantitatively, but we must appreciate that whichever
of us is the better partner contributes more qualitatively.'

'"To this, Socrates, my wife replied: 'What assistance can I be
to you? What can *I* do? It's all up to you: my mother told me that
my job was to be responsible.'

'"'Yes, my dear, of course,' I said. 'My father gave me the same
advice. But you should know that responsible people of either
sex should act in such a way as to ensure that their property is
in the best possible condition and is increased as much as fair and
honest dealings permit.'

'"'And what can I do to increase our estate?' asked my wife.
'Can you see anything I can do?'

'"'Yes, indeed I can,' I replied. 'You can try to utilize to the best
of your ability the talents which the gods have implanted in you
and society approves.'

'"'What talents do you mean?' she asked.

'"'Ones which, in my opinion,' I said, 'are far from worthless—
unless the jobs over which the queen bee of a hive presides are
worthless! I'll tell you what I'm getting at, my dear. I think that
the gods exercised especially acute discernment in establishing
the particular pairing which is called "male and female", to ensure that, when the partners cooperate, such a pair may be of the

utmost mutual benefit. In the first place, this pairing with each other is established as a procreative unit so that animal species might not die out. In the second place, human beings, at any rate, are supplied with the means to have supporters in their old age as a result of this pairing. In the third place, human life, unlike that of other animals, which live in the open, obviously requires shelter.

Indoor and Outdoor Tasks

But if people are to have something to store in this shelter, then they need someone to work out in the open: ploughing, sowing, planting and pasturing are all open-air jobs, and they are the sources of the necessities of life. Now, when these necessities have been brought under cover, then in turn there is a need for someone to keep them safe and to do the jobs for which shelter is required. Looking after new-born children requires shelter, as does making bread from corn and clothes from wool.

'"'Since both of these domains—indoor and outdoor—require work and attention, then God, as I see it, directly made woman's nature suitable for the indoor jobs and tasks, and man's nature suitable for the outdoor ones. For he made the masculine body and mind more capable of enduring cold and heat and travel and military expeditions, which implies that he ordained the outdoor work for man; and God seems to me to have assigned the indoor work to woman, since he made the female body less capable in these respects. And knowing that he had made it the woman's natural job to feed new-born children, he apportioned to her a greater facility for loving new-born infants than he did to man. And because he had assigned to the woman the work of looking after the stores, God, recognizing that timidity is no disadvantage in such work, gave a larger share of fearfulness to woman than he did to man. And knowing that it would also be necessary for the one who does the outdoor work to provide protection against potential wrongdoers, he gave him a greater share of courage. But because both sexes need to give as well as receive, he shared memory and awareness between them both, and consequently you wouldn't be able to say whether the male or the female sex has more of these. He also shared between them both the ability to be suitably responsible, and made it the right of whichever of them, the man or the woman, is better at this to reap more of its benefits. In so far as the two sexes have different natural talents, their need for each other is greater and their pairing is mutually more beneficial, because the one has the abilities the other lacks.

'"So, my dear,' I said, 'we must recognize what God has assigned to each of us, and try our hardest to carry through our respective responsibilities. Society approves of this too, since it pairs a man and a woman together. Just as God has made men and women share in procreation, so society makes them share in estate-management. Moreover, where God has implanted in either sex greater ability, there custom gives its blessing. For it is better for the woman to stay indoors than to go out, but it is more reprehensible for the man to stay indoors than to look after the outside work. And if a man acts contrary to the talents God has implanted in him, then the chances are that the gods notice his disobedience and punish him for neglecting his own duties or doing the woman's work. And I think,' I concluded, 'that the queen bee works away at similar tasks as God has assigned her.'

'"How are the queen bee's tasks similar to the ones I should do?' asked my wife.

'"In that although she stays in the hive,' I replied, 'she doesn't allow the bees to be idle: those whose duty it is to work outside she sends out to their work. She also acquaints herself with everything that every bee brings into the hive, receives it and keeps it safe until it is required; when the time comes for it to be used, she distributes a fair proportion to each bee. She also oversees the construction of the honeycomb in the hive, making sure that it is constructed correctly and quickly; and she looks after the growing brood, making sure that it reaches maturity. When it does so and the youngsters are capable of working, she sends them out to found a colony, with a queen to rule the company.'

'"So I too will be required to do these things?' asked my wife.

Her Wifely Duties

'"Yes,' I said. 'You will have to stay indoors and send out the servants who have outdoor jobs, and oversee those with indoor jobs. You must receive the produce that is brought in from outside and distribute as much of it as needs dispensing; but as for the proportion of it which needs putting on one side, you must look ahead and make sure that the outgoings assigned for the year are not dispensed in a month. When wool is brought in to you, you must try to make certain that those who need clothes get them. And you must try to ensure that the gram is made into edible provisions. One of your responsibilities, however,' I added, 'will probably seem rather unpleasant: when any servant is ill, you must make sure that he is thoroughly looked after.'

'"'No, no!' said my wife. 'That will be quite the opposite of un-pleasant, provided that those who are well looked after turn out to be grateful and to grow in their loyalty.'

'"I was delighted at this reply of hers. So I said, 'It is attentive actions like these on the part of the queen in the hive too which make the attitude of the bees towards her such that, when she leaves the hive, not a single bee thinks of abandoning her, but they all go with her. Don't you think, my dear, that such actions are the reason for this?'

'"'I would think it likely,' said my wife, 'that the actions of a leader like the queen bee are more applicable to you than to me. My storage and distribution of things indoors would look pretty absurd, I think, if *you* weren't trying to make sure that produce is brought in from outside.'

'"'On the other hand,' I replied, 'my bringing produce in would look absurd without someone to keep what was brought in safe! Don't you see how those who pour water into a leaky jar, as the proverb puts it, are pitied for their useless effort?'

'"'Yes, and pity is what they deserve, of course,' said my wife, 'for doing it.'

'"'Anyway,' I said, 'some of your specific responsibilities will be gratifying, such as getting a servant who is ignorant of spin-ning, teaching it to her and doubling her value to you; or getting one who is ignorant of housekeeping and service, teaching her to be a reliable servant, and ending up with her being of ines-timable value; or having the right to reward those in your house-hold who are disciplined and helpful, and to punish anyone who turns out to be bad. And the most gratifying thing of all will be if you turn out to be better than me, and make me your servant. This will mean that you need not worry that, as the years pass, you will have less standing in the household; instead you will have grounds for believing that, as you grow older, you will have me standing in the household, in proportion to the increase in your value to me as a partner and to our children as a protector of the home. For it is virtue rather than the physical beauty of youth that increases true goodness in human life.'

'"That, Socrates, as near as I can remember, was my first conversation with her."

Basic Forms of Classical Dress

Iris Brooke

Most of the clothes worn in ancient Greece (as well as in numerous other Mediterranean lands, which copied Greek dress to one degree or another between about 600 B.C. and A.D. 200) fell into a few simple, basic forms. Each could be worn in a number of different variations and styles, depending on the situation and/or the wearer's personal tastes. This well-informed overview of the main Greek garments is by former Bristol University scholar Iris Brooke, who meticulously studied thousands of vase paintings in Greece, as well as descriptions of clothes in ancient Greek literature, including the epic poem the *Odyssey,* by the famous Greek poet Homer.

G enerally speaking, classic costume as worn from the Attic period [i.e., the age of Classical Athens, about 500–300 B.C.] until the time of the Roman Empire was comparatively simple, although there is a rich variety of superficial small garments that tend to complicate the general effect. The accepted terms of definition applied to the *chiton*, or main dress, are Doric and Ionic; this divides them according to two of the main orders in architecture, which were developed by the two leading racial groups, Ionian Greeks and Dorian Greeks. The Doric was severely simple; the Ionic a trifle more complicated, as indeed the Ionic is in every sense.

The Simple Chiton

Taking the Doric chiton first, we find that it was a straight, unsewn piece of material, wrapped around the body and pinned on the shoulders. The material could be of almost any width, from a yard up to about three yards, but it was probably not wider than three yards.

Iris Brooke, *Costume in Greek Classic Drama*. London: Methuen, 1962. Copyright © 1962 by Iris Brooke. Reproduced by permission.

The width of the woven material formed the line from neck to hem, and the length of the material went round the body. Therefore, the wider the fabric the longer the gown. Thus whenever Homer mentions "double-width" he means that the robe was luxuriously long, possibly even trailing on the ground. The method of wearing it differed only in the adjustment of the width to suit the wearer. If the material is folded in half and two pins inserted half a yard from either end, the head can then be put through the space between the pins and the chiton will fall from the shoulders suspended by the pins, open at the right side with a folded loop under the left arm. A girdle holds the garment in position. This is the simplest form and is worn by working and fighting men and sometimes by serving women. The more usual feminine, decorative style is to fold over the top of the chiton before inserting the pins so that a hanging drapery falls from the pins and shows the (probably decorated) top or border of the material hanging over the chest like a collar.

The placing of the girdle is an entirely personal matter. Should the chiton be very long, which fashion normally occurs for women only, there may be two girdles worn, one high up under the breasts, and one at the waist. The extra material swags out under the lower girdle. Generally speaking, the Doric version is simple. The pins were long and pointed like little daggers with a decorated end. Apparently they were, on occasion, used as such, and served in emergencies as small weapons of defence.

More Stylish Chitons

The Ionic chiton is much fuller than the Doric (i.e. the material has the same width but is longer), and is sewn up like a vast unshaped skirt. To put it on, one of the open edges should be pinned at regular intervals leaving a slightly larger interval for the head to go through. The hands are then put through between the last pin at each end and the fold in the fabric. This will form a sort of long sleeve with the pins decorating the arm and permitting the material to fall open between them, showing the bare arm. About five yards of length is required to give the right effect. Again, it can be girdled as desired. The girdle itself will help to pleat the skirt. . . .

We can assume that the majority of these chitons were originally made from very fine wool. This would give them the full beauty of the softly flowing draperies. . . .

These Ionic chitons were frequently pleated. The pleating could have been done in a manner similar to broomstick pleating, which is still the most economical method of pleating real silk. The silk is folded tightly when wet and wound around a straight stick till it is dry; when dry, the pleats remain in place until the material is washed again. This could only be done with a perfectly straight length of material with no flares or cutting on the cross because of the stretching involved. If this very simple method had been used in the fifth century it would account for the arrangement of groups of little pleats, and again groups of larger ones, a form which is so very effective in the clear calligraphic drawings on Greek vases.

No doubt many of the lovely drawings that fascinate one by their pleated fantasy were not so exaggerated as we might believe from looking at them. One little figure in the British Museum showing Theseus slaying the Minotaur has fascinated me for many years because of the pleated magnificence of his chiton. Because of this figure an experiment in broomstick pleating was carried out. A length of material about six yards long and forty-two inches wide was used. When this came off the broom it was easy to handle. The top could be turned down over a cord arranged around the shoulders, and after a deal of fiddling it was discovered that as long as there was sufficient material, the chevron edge could be achieved and pinned into place on the cord, so that however much movement was carried out the hemline remained the same, fuller wherever it was lifted than at its deeper points. . . .

A description of what sounds uncommonly like an Ionic chiton can be found in Book XVIII of the *Odyssey*, when Penelope is brought gifts from her suitors. Whether this particular gown was known in Homer's time is debatable, but this indicates so very clearly something of the sort that it would seem to fit very well and might have been a copyist's idea: ". . . For Antinous they brought a long embroidered robe of the most beautiful material on which were fixed a dozen golden brooches, each fitted with a curved sheath for the pin". The twelve golden brooches would seem to be the six pins which appear on each arm. These pins were sheathed, an important improvement on the original dagger type of pin; they were also already on the robe, so that in a sense it was made up and therefore a finished garment ready to wear. . . .

The Great-Cloak

Over the chiton was worn a cloak some four or five yards long and about a yard in width. This is known as an *himation* and was arranged and decorated in a variety of styles. The ends were decorated and quite often had a fringe or tassels or some small weight of beads attached at the corners, so that in movement the weight swung away from the body and emphasized the pattern of the border design. It was worn, as all the garments were, by both men and women. There was no distinctive garment peculiar to either sex, though a version of the himation with the lower edge woven in points and the upper edge pleated on to a band worn under one arm and fastened on the opposite shoulder seems to appear far more frequently on women than it does on men. This highly decorative pleated himation is nearly always represented as one of [the war goddess] Athene's garments, also those of queens and other noble women. Its shape lends itself readily to sculpture and the borders of decoration make a fine pattern on the figured vases. When the himation is worn with the chevron edge the pleating at once becomes something of a mystery. Various views have been expressed as to the exact way in which this was attached to the band at the top. Such a band was arranged from one shoulder, across the breast and under the other arm and back to the shoulder again. The himation was attached to this and was fastened with a row of pins down the arm in much the same manner as the Ionic chiton. The effect was both graceful and decorative, for the points hanging from the arm seem to have been weighted so that they were dragged straight in movement. These himations are always pleated although the pleats do not appear to be pressed. Sometimes the whole length resembled an accordion pleating in that each pleat was exactly the same distance away from its neighbour; at other times a cluster of little pleats seems to have been attached at certain intervals to the band that encircles the body. In many cases the top of the pleated material is free and folds over the band in a series of decorative scallops. It appears that these himations are arranged with geometrical care. The arrangement is similar to the cartridge pleating used in the time of Henry VIII, when vast amounts of woollen fabric were folded into regularly spaced loops and each loop left free. From both drawings and sculpture it looks as if the place where the attachment was made was some five or six inches from the top edge of the material. If, as is so often the case, the material had a border, this border would hang down over the band forming the decorative scallops already referred to above. The chevron edge is also decorated with some sort of design, not necessarily similar to that at the top.

There are literally dozens of different arrangements of the himation, and it would seem impossible to lay down any definite laws as to the exact shape and manner in which it is worn on some of the sculptured figures. Probably many of the lovely, intricate draperies show artistic licence, and the curious manner in which such draperies flow defies a practical analysis.

The normal purpose of the himation or great-cloak was as a protection from the elements, so that during the winter the himation became as valuable to the Greeks as the plaid to a Scotsman, and the whole figure can be swathed in its voluminous folds.

Yet another form of cloak is the *chlamys*, a short and generally much briefer affair, which is sometimes shown tied round the body under one arm and round the waist, or just buckled on one shoulder, the ends falling straight. The chlamys was used chiefly by soldiers and messengers.

One more garment which had various uses was known as the *peplos*. This could have been a tunic woven straight on the loom in the manner already described, but there are obvious examples which look as if they were made up with a shoulder seam and embroidered neckband. The difficulty is that often some such neckbands, holding the pleats or gathers in place, appear also on the chiton. For the sake of clarity in description . . . "peplos". . . is a perfectly adequate term for the little tunics that are worn over a chiton for warmth or decoration, and it can also apply to many of the tunics that are worn by servants and fighting men. It can be made with or without sleeves.

This inventory, then, completes the fundamental [ancient Greek] garments with which we are concerned.

Food and Dining

Andrew Dalby

According to Andrew Dalby, an expert on ancient Greek foods and eating customs, the Greeks ate not only at home, but also in town halls and at outdoor public sacrifices. Describing eating at home, he tells how men sometimes gave dinner parties for their male friends, while the women of the house often ate separately. Dalby also lists the most common foods eaten by average Greeks, including their desserts.

Families often must have eaten at home, but only the briefest descriptions are to be found. If sacrificing and eating fresh meat, families might eat at shrines. . . . Men formed dining clubs which could assume political importance: evidence for them comes from historical sources and occasional inscriptions, but there is no full description of such a dinner. The state acted as celebrant at general religious festivals and as host for entertainments at the town hall. . . . Workers, soldiers and those engaged in some communal activities ate away from home, these 'working' meals sometimes being provided for them. . . . Travellers who could not call on acquaintances had to eat at inns. Some members of a household spent the whole day away from home, taking food with them if there was to be no communal ration. . . . Women, household slaves and children then certainly ate independently of their menfolk. Women lunched with one another, as we have seen, though respectable women did not go out to dinner in the evening.

Meal times are variable, but a midday meal was usually called *áriston*, 'lunch' . . . and an evening meal *deîpnon*, 'dinner'. The latter was perhaps typically the biggest meal of the day, and for some the only meal.

Throwing a Dinner Party

Families who were sacrificing, especially if celebrating such an event as a betrothal or wedding, but on other occasions too, invited guests to their meal. Men of the socially approved age . . .

Andrew Dalby, *Siren Feasts: A History of Food and Gastronomy in Greece*. New York: Routledge, 1996. Copyright © 1996 by Andrew Dalby. Reproduced by permission of the publisher.

pursued courtship by entertaining. Men entertained male guests at home, and might also celebrate some public achievement, athletic or political, with a sacrificial dinner or a party for friends. *Hetairaí* [high-class prostitutes], and other women not of the proper status to be citizens' wives, might be guests at such entertainments, at home or at a shrine. These were evening and night activities: a dinner might become a drinking party, a *pótos,* or one more eleaborate and organised, a *sympósion*. . . . But dinner parties and drinking parties were surely (in Athens as in most societies) less ubiquitous than their frequent occurrence in memoirs and fiction would suggest. . . .

When no strange men were in the house, women need not retreat to 'women's quarters': they could lunch at leisure, indoors or in a courtyard. But the classical Athenian house, and the conviviality within it, were very inaccessible to the uninvited visitor. Women at home were invisible to law-abiding outsiders. House doors were commonly locked, and interiors divided into several rooms. One of these was the *andrón*, the 'dining room'. . . . It was in this room, customarily, that men entertained others to meals and drinking parties at home. Its ground plan was laid out to accommodate a certain number of couches around the walls. *Andrônes* can be recognised archaeologically by the location of the door (always off-centre), by the length of the walls (so many couch lengths plus one couch width) and often by floor details recognisably linked to the intended placing of couches and tables. They were one-purpose rooms, more clearly so than any other room in normal houses; how frequently they were used is quite unknown. Women of respectable Athenian households did not come into contact with male guests and had no reason to enter the *andrón* when it was in use. In all the narratives of men's dinners and *sympósia* from the fifth and fourth centuries there is not one certain indication of the presence of a woman of the household, and there are several explicit signs that they were elsewhere.

Similar rooms to these *andrônes* are found in certain municipal buildings, which are thus identified as *prytanêia*—places for municipal eating—and in buildings at shrines. But many country shrines had no buildings, and certainly vase-paintings suggest that open air meals, otherwise resembling meals in dining rooms, were quite imaginable; a few literary references, scattered in time and place, and one or two paintings from Pompeii, imply that an awning (often translated 'tent') might be a regular amenity.

The high Greek dining couch was a specialised piece of furniture. It is a standard feature of vase-paintings of banquets and must have been standard in the purpose-built dining rooms just described. On the vase-paintings, with few exceptions, the rule is one diner per couch: a second person on a couch will be a woman (or occasionally a beardless young man) often offering the male diner some more or less intimate service or performing it. But not all lived in such style as to own a house with a room dedicated to dining; not all could have afforded to own all those couches. The less well-off, when they entertained, are perhaps more likely than the rich to have done so at shrines, and to have taken rugs and cushions with them. . . .

We know that at Athenian dinner parties the guests were limited in number. It is easy to count the couches that would fit in the purpose-built dining rooms of Attica . . . whether private, municipal or religious: that was exactly how the size of a reception room was customarily measured. Seven couches was a common size; five to eleven couches was the usual range, or in other words hardly more than twenty participants. . . . The intimate scale was part of the nature of Greek dining and entertainment, and was built in architecturally, for in the larger of known dining rooms the layout would have produced the effect of two to four groups dining or drinking simultaneously. . . .

The picture that can be drawn of dining and festivity in other classical Greek cities is by no means so complete as the Athenian. Athenians were, however, sufficiently impressed by the contrast between their own way of life and that of the Spartans to describe the latter relatively fully. The evidence is not straightforward, however. We can read satire on Sparta and its ways, from a city that was always Sparta's rival and frequently its enemy; also we can read strong praise, from Plato and Xenophon, philosophers and moralists whose admiration for Spartan discipline and education was almost unbounded. A fictional Spartan speaks:

> Still, I think the lawgiver at Sparta was right to enjoin the avoidance of pleasures. . . . The custom that makes men fall deepest into great pleasures and improprieties and into all foolishness, this has been ejected by our law from every part of the country: nei-

ther in the fields, nor in the towns that the Spartiates control, will you see a *sympósion* and all that goes with it to incite men to pleasure. There is not a man who would not punish with the greatest severity a drunken reveller; he would not get away even if a festival of Dionysus were his excuse—like the time when I saw [drunken revellers] on carts in your country [Athens], while at Taras, our own colony, I watched the whole city getting drunk at the Dionysia. There is none of that with us.

(Plato, *Laws* 636c–637c)

The full citizens, the Spartiates, were above over-indulgence in food and drink, or so it was claimed. But the principal difference in this field between Sparta and Athens was that whereas the communal or municipal dining of Athenians seems (to judge from surviving literature) to have been of little importance, male Spartiates dined in common all the time. Where and in what circumstances their womenfolk ate, no one knows. Communal meals, *syssítia*, were by no means unique to Sparta. Cretan cities, close to Sparta in dialect, were also close in social customs and there too men ate communally. . . .

Outlandish though they seemed to other Greeks . . . from our perspective the customs of Sparta can be seen to belong to the same spectrum as those of Athens. Athenians, like Spartans, had fixed opinions on dining together, on equal contribution to hospitality, on the separation of the sexes, on the ages at which boys began to dine as men. Spartans, like Athenians, celebrated religious occasions with food, drink, music and dance, as we know not only from the early poetry of Aleman but also from descriptions of what were evidently well-established festivals dating from the classical period or soon after it.

But every Greek city was different from every other in government, in laws, in religious observance and in other customs. Sacrifice and food preparation were naturally a major source of income at places of pilgrimage and festival. Delians were nicknamed *eleodytai*, 'table-divers', and . . . Elis, where Olympia stood, was said to be the origin of a school of cooks. Distinctions in food behaviour are among the most quickly noticed of all social peculiarities. Greeks noticed such differences among themselves: the women of Miletus, for example, who 'are not to share food with their husbands nor to call their own husbands by name' (Herodotus, *Histories* 1.146.3).

Common Foods

They also noticed how they were differentiated from other peoples—from 'barbarians'—by food customs, food choices and food avoidances. Herodotus was told that after sacrifice in Egyptian temples the animal's head would be cut off, cursed and if there was a market at hand with Greek traders, sold to them. If there was not, it would be thrown in the river. . . .

Greeks themselves admitted to few food avoidances, though they considered dolphins sacred, were doubtful of turtle and tortoise, seldom ate dog and very seldom horse. Of animals that were eaten at all, nearly all parts were considered acceptable food. . . . Some Greeks, though not all, ate brain; Pythagoras, it was later said, included heart among his odd list of forbidden foods. . . .

Lentils, barley and wheat formed the staple foods (*sîtos*: 'food, staple food, army food supply') of classical Greece: the lentils as soup, the barley as a mash or biscuit, the wheat as loaves, though both of the cereals could also be prepared as gruel or porridge. In addition to the older traditional forms in which these staples were eaten, sweet cakes multiplied in classical menus. Wheat . . . did not grow well in most parts of Greece and was the most expensive and the most unreliable of the three staples. Lentils and barley had been known in Greece even earlier than wheat: they were available almost everywhere. . . .

With these staples were eaten . . . vegetables, cheese, eggs, fish (fresh, salted or dried), and less frequently meat. In classical Greece the fresh meat of domestic animals formed a sacrifice, butchered with appropriate religious ritual. But the eating of meat once sacrificed, including the eating of offal and sausages, required no further ceremony. The domestic animals that were most commonly eaten—sheep, goats and pigs—had a long prehistory in Greece. Small and large game birds supplemented the native domesticated quail and the domestic fowl. . . . Cheese (in Greece normally sheep's and goats' milk cheese) had long been made. The number of species of vegetables in use had gradually grown. The number of species of fish that were exploited no doubt remained fairly constant once deep-sea fishing had become a common practice. . . .

To this structure, when meals were at their most elaborate, there were many supplements. Appetisers, not different in kind from the usual relishes but selected from those that had the most piquant flavour, preceded the meal. Wreaths and perfumes were distributed among guests as they gathered.

After the meal, wine, *oînos*, was drunk, a single taste of un-mixed wine at the moment of the libation, followed by plenty of wine mixed with water. Now clean tables—'second tables'—were brought, on which cakes, sweets, nuts and fresh and dried fruit were served to accompany the wine. These delicacies were called *tragémata*, 'what one chews alongside wine' (a convenient trans-lation is 'dessert'). . . .

One of the two most important changes in the diet of Greece since early neolithic times has been the introduction of wine: it has for at least the last three millennia been the customary drink of the country, often heavily diluted with water. The other has been the cultivation and regular use of olives. Wild forms of both grape and olive were found and probably used earlier in Greece, but the newly cultivated grape and olive of later prehistoric times were of enormous potential importance to the diet. Both pro-vided cooking media and flavourings, the olive with its oil, the grape with its juice both unfermented and fermented into wine. It is a challenging hint of conservatism at the centre of the menu that grape, wine and olive were not visibly present in the main course of a classical Greek meal. Whatever the use of olive oil in cooking, and as a medium for sauces, olives themselves were eaten only before the meal as an appetiser. Whatever the use of must and wine in cooking, wine was served to diners only after they had eaten, and raisins also appeared then, with the second tables. And in general the lists of *propómata*, 'appetisers', and of *tragémata* that can be extracted from the writings of comic poets and dieticians alike show a readiness to innovate that was not nearly so evident with the staple diet and its chief accompani-ments in the main course.

Meat was eaten 'less frequently'. How frequently is 'less fre-quently'? The balance is difficult to judge. . . . Although the ev-idence is not strong, it is likely that vegetables, fish and perhaps cheese, and not meat, accompanied the majority of meals in Greece for many millennia.

Education in Ancient Athens

Joint Association of Classical Teachers

It is likely, though not certain, that schools and teachers in most of the larger and many of the smaller city-states of classical Greece resembled those in Athens, from which most of the surviving evidence about Greek education derives. (The major exception was Sparta, which placed an inordinate emphasis on military training for young men.) This summary of ancient Greek education was compiled by a panel of college professors known as the Joint Association of Classical Teachers.

In Athens, as in almost all other Greek states with the notable exception of Sparta, education was a private affair, arranged and paid for by parents who were not legally compelled to have their children formally educated. Teachers were often of low status and badly paid. . . . Deductions [were made] from the teacher's pay if the child is absent through illness. Schools were run from private houses or rooms attached to a public or private training-ground (*palaistra*) which could be used for physical education. Boys began to attend school from about the age of seven, or earlier if the family was rich.

Reading and Writing

There were three main areas of education: basic literacy (and perhaps arithmetic), music, and physical education. Some schools offered training in all three, but parents might choose different teachers for the individual subjects. Basic literacy, which was greatly facilitated by the Greeks' invention of a fully phonetic alphabet script, was taught by the *grammatistēs*. Despite his low status, his job was fundamentally important, since many aspects of the democracy depended for their efficient functioning on at least a rudimentary knowledge of reading and writing. Once a boy

Joint Association of Classical Teachers, *The World of Athens*. New York: Cambridge University Press, 1984. Copyright © 1984 by Cambridge University Press. Reproduced by permission.

could read he was sent Homer and other poets, often to learn by heart and recite from memory. As Plato puts it:

> When a boy knows his letters and is ready to proceed from the spoken to the written word, his teachers set him down at his desk and make him read the works of the great poets and learn them by heart; there he finds plenty of good advice, and many stories and much praise and glorification of great men of the past, which encourage him to admire and imitate them and to model himself on them. (Plato, *Protagoras* 325e–326a)

Monotonously repetitive exercises on wax tablets were used to practise writing, and some of the few vase paintings of school scenes show the teacher wielding a sandal to encourage the others. There were, nevertheless, Athenian illiterates. The most famous . . . story concerns the one who asked [the general and politician] Aristeides to write his own name on a potsherd to get him ostracised [banished], because he was sick of hearing Aristeides constantly praised for being just.

Music and Athletics

The music teacher instructed boys in singing and in playing the *aulos* or lyre. Perhaps not all children had a very extensive musical education, since [the comic playwright] Aristophanes represents the ability to play the lyre as a mark of the cultured gentleman. But music was certainly important to people at all levels of Athenian society. Plato, indeed, took its moral significance so seriously that he banned all but one of the musical modes from his utopian state. Music played a large part in many festivals, above all the Dionysia [dedicated to the god Dionysos] with its choral lyrics in tragedy and comedy and its contests between choruses of both men and boys in the singing of dithyrambs (songs in honour of Dionysos). These choral contests point to the close connection between music and poetry at Athens; even narrative poetry like Homer's *Iliad* and *Odyssey* was recited to musical accompaniment. Equally close was the link between music and dancing: *khoros* is the Greek for 'a dance' as well as 'a chorus'. For the well-to-do musical entertainment was an integral part of the private symposium too.

Physical training was supervised by a *paidotribēs*, who gave instruction in running, long jump, throwing the javelin and discus, boxing and wrestling. Since Greek *poleis* [city-states] depended for their survival on their citizen troops, physical skills and fitness were vital. For this purpose Athens provided public gymnasia (so called because the Greeks exercised there *gumnoi*, 'stark naked') in addition to the many *palaistrai*. These were general meeting-places and used for a variety of purposes besides physical exercise; Plato's Academy, for example, takes its name from its location within the gymnasium of Akademos (or Hekademos).

Physical training did not only have a utilitarian military end in view. Athletic excellence was one of the most important fields in which the Greeks expressed their essentially competitive value-system. Greatest renown was accorded to the victors in the Panhellenic festivals, but not far behind these in prestige came the Panathenaic (All-Athenian) Games, which was the greatest of the local festivals. During these celebrations, contests in honour of the gods were held, at first in running, but later in other sports and in music and poetry too. Contestants came from all over the far-flung Greek world, and the victors covered not only themselves but their cities in glory.

The Sophists

At Athens the length of a child's formal education varied according to the means and outlook of his parents; there was no school-leaving age. In his pamphlet on the social system of Sparta [the Athenian soldier and historian] Xenophon assumes that children elsewhere were not normally educated beyond childhood; and though an Athenian by birth and upbringing, Xenophon praises Sparta to the skies for its comprehensive educational curriculum that was obligatory for boys from the age of seven right up to adulthood. What Xenophon keeps very quiet about was the almost exclusively physical and martial character of Spartan education. There was nothing corresponding to secondary, let alone higher, education in this state, because there was no need for it in a warrior society. But at Athens, especially after the Persian Wars, new social and political needs created the demand for new kinds of education, and the demand was satisfied by men known—often derogatorily—as 'sophists'.

A *sophistēs* originally meant simply a sage or wise man. . . . But already by the end of the fifth century *sophistēs* had acquired the pejorative [negative] sense from which we derive our 'sophistical' and 'sophistry'. On this hostile view a sophist was a charlatan, a clever-clever verbal trickster whose stock-in-trade was to make the worse seem the better argument. To compound his felony (as the critics saw it) the sophist charged a fat fee to his pupils in return for corrupting their moral sense and turning them into immoral know-it-alls kicking over the traces of established convention.

Persuasion (*peithō*) is the nub of the matter. In an era of rapid political, economic and social change, political success no longer depended simply on a family name and glory won in battle but also, and above all, on the power of persuasive speech in *ekklēsia* [assembly] and lawcourt. He who by skilful rhetoric could persuade mass audiences of Athenians to his viewpoint became a leader (*prostatēs*) of the Athenian democracy.

Our evidence on the sophists and their teaching is unfortunately very one-sided. It comes almost entirely from their opponents, especially Plato. Only a handful of fragments of original sophistic writings has survived verbatim from antiquity. Yet even Plato, for all his intellectual brilliance and verbal dexterity, cannot entirely hide the fact that the sophists' teaching filled a serious gap. In two of his dialogues the question of why the young have failed to match up to their famous fathers is explicitly raised in terms of their defective education. Indeed, Plato's own philosophical achievement is inexplicable unless the contribution of the sophists is taken into account.

What the sophists provided was in effect a higher education for the sons of the rich. Though the sophists did not form a single school, the issue that lay at the heart of their teaching was *aretē*, 'goodness' or 'excellence'. The sophists claimed both to know what *aretē* was in any given field, whether politics, religion or private morality, and to be able to teach that *aretē* to their pupils. Their opponents claimed either, like Plato, that *aretē* was not teachable or, like Aristophanes in agreement with Plato, that their versions of *aretē* were immoral and wrong. It seemed to them and to many ordinary Athenians that the traditional view of morality—whereby universal standards of human behaviour were sanctioned by the gods—was threatened by the sophists' ability to present apparently convincing arguments on both sides of any moral issue.

The First Universities

Almost all the sophists who taught in Athens were foreigners, men like Protagoras of Abdera and Hippias of Elis (a sophist of prodigious memory and learning). This is one reason why Aristophanes in his *Clouds* chose to attack Socrates as the representative of all the sophists, since Socrates was an Athenian citizen and so could be identified as a more immediate threat by an Athenian audience. Plato vehemently denied that his revered master was a sophist, partly on the technical ground that he did not accept pay from his pupils. . . .

Socrates' condemnation did not mean the end of higher education in Athens. Far from it. At some time in the 390s [the Greek orator] Isokrates set up the first 'university' at Athens, essentially a school of advanced rhetoric, and his example was soon followed by Plato and his more philosophically based Academy. However, these institutes of higher learning no longer occupied the centre of the Athenian political stage in the way that the sophists had done, on occasions, during the latter part of the fifth century.

Yet even if these institutions were not as central to the political life of Athens as individual thinkers had been in the fifth century, they still engaged fiercely in debates between themselves. Isokrates attacked both the sophists for their verbal quibbling and Plato for his 'head-in-the-clouds' attitude to philosophy, and dedicated his own school to the principle of utility in education. The debate is still with us. In the following passage (*c.* 370), Isokrates attacks philosophers for their useless speculations:

> There are some who are very proud of their ability to formulate an absurd and paradoxical proposition and then make a tolerable defence of it. There are men who have spent their lives saying that it is impossible to make or to deny a false statement or to argue on both sides of the same question; there are others who maintain that courage and wisdom and justice are all the same, that we are not born with any of them but that they are all the concern of a single kind of knowledge; and there are still others who waste time on disputes which are quite useless and liable to get their pupils into trouble . . . They ought to give up this hairsplitting pedantry which pretends to find in verbal argument proof of absurdities which have in practice long been refuted, and turn to the real world and give their pupils instruction in the practicalities of public affairs and some experitise in them. They should

remember that it is much better to be able to form a reasonable judgement about practical affairs than to have any amount of precise but useless knowledge, and that it is better to have a marginal superiority in affairs of importance than to excel in detailed knowledge of no consequence.

The truth is that they care for nothing except making money out of the young. This is what their so-called philosophy with its concern with disputation for its own sake can do. For the young, who give little thought to private or public affairs, particularly enjoy completely pointless argument. One can well forgive them for that, for they have always been inclined to extremes and taken in by startling novelties. (Isokrates, *Helen* 1ff.)

Communal and Social Activities

CHAPTER 2

Chapter Preface

Like private life, communal and social activities in ancient Greece were strongly guided by tradition. Social events were almost always highly stimulating and enriching experiences. First, there was community worship, in which most members of the community got together during annual religious festivals and prayed and sacrificed to the gods—especially to the city's own patron deity, who was thought to watch over and protect the community. The gods, as pictured by master poets and storytellers like Homer and Hesiod, were thought to be human-like beings with faults and problems much like those of people; the main difference was that the gods possessed vastly greater power than humans.

Especially important in Greek communities, particularly democracies such as Athens (the world's first), was participation in political affairs. These included assembly meetings of the male citizens to choose leaders and/or decide on community laws and policies. Men also made up the large juries that heard cases brought to trial. These cases ranged from simple complaints about the location of property lines to capital offenses such as murder and treason. There were no professional lawyers, so the accused had to defend himself. The accused, however, was allowed to have a professional speechwriter compose his court presentation.

Other vital communal activities included banking and local industries. Manufacture and trade comprised the financial backbone of a Greek city-state, as goods made in that community were both used locally and exported to other cities, while other goods were imported from those cities. To help keep the commercial markets healthy and viable, merchants and tradesmen regularly borrowed money from bankers, who made their own livings from the interest they charged.

No less important to the communal life of Greek communities than religious worship, politics, and trade was athletics. Greeks everywhere so revered and looked forward to the Olympic Games (held every four years at Olympia, in southern Greece) that they declared temporary truces in wars to ensure that athletes and spectators could make the journey to the games safely. And in many cities a local man who won an event at Olympia was hailed as a hometown hero and provided with free meals for the rest of his days.

How the World and Gods Came to Be

Hesiod

Like other world religions, that of the ancient Greeks had its creation stories, telling how the world and gods came to be. The most detailed and popular was that of the eighth-century B.C. Boeotian poet Hesiod in his *Theogony,* which translates roughly as *The Genealogy of the Gods.* In the following excerpts (translated by Rhoda A. Hendricks), he begins with formless chaos, as most creation myths do. Springing from chaos, he envisions natural forces and kinds of physical matter, such as earth and sea, taking the form of beings who can reason and reproduce. Thus, Gaea, the Earth, soon mates with Uranus, the Sky or Heavens, and give rise to Cyclopes and other giants and monsters, as well as the first race of gods, the Titans. The leading Titan, Cronus, marries his sister, Rhea, and they produce the first group of Olympian gods, including Zeus. Hesiod then proceeds to give an exciting account of the devastating war between these two divine races, as well as an atmospheric description of Tartarus, comprising the darkest reaches of the Underworld.

First of all Chaos came into being, and then Gaea, the broad Earth, the ever certain support of all the deathless gods who dwell on the summit of snowy Olympus, and also dark Tartarus in the innermost part of the broad-pathed earth, and also Eros [the power of love and sexual union], the fairest of the immortal gods, who relaxes the limbs and overpowers the resolution and thoughtful determination in the hearts of all the gods and all mankind.

From Chaos came both Erebus [Darkness] and Nyx, the black Night, and of Nyx there were born Aether and Hemera, the Day, whom she bore to Erebus in a union of love. And Gaea first of all brought forth an equal to herself, Uranus, the starry Heaven,

Hesiod, *Classical Gods and Heros: Myths as Told by Ancient Authors,* translated and edited by Rhonda A. Hendricks. New York: Morrow Quill, 1974. Copyright © 1974 by Rhonda A. Hendricks. Reproduced by permission of the publisher.

to cover her about on all sides and to be an ever certain dwelling place for the blessed gods.

Gaea also brought forth far-reaching Hills, the pleasant homes of the goddess Nymphs, who dwell in the wooded valleys of the hills. Without the delights of love, she also gave birth to the barren sea, Pontus, with his swelling waves. But later she lay with Uranus and bore [the Titans, including] deep-eddying Oceanus, Hyperion, and Iapetus, also Theia and Rhea, and Themis and Mnemosyne, and gold-crowned Phoebe and lovely Tethys. After them the youngest was born, the wily Cronus, the most dreadful of her children, and he hated his vigorous father.

In addition, she gave birth to the Cyclopes [giants], who possess mighty hearts, Brontes and Steropes and also strong-minded Arges, who gave thunder to Zeus and forged the thunderbolt. They were like the gods in all other respects, but a single eye was set in the middle of their foreheads. They were given the name Cyclopes, because indeed one round eye was set in their foreheads. Strength and force and craftiness were in their deeds.

Three other sons were also born of Gaea and Uranus, huge and strong [monsters named] Cottus and Briareus and Gyges, overpowering offspring. A hundred arms rose from their shoulders, and each one had fifty heads growing out of his shoulders, set upon sturdy limbs, and the physical strength in their great frames was mighty and dreadful. They were the most terrible of the children born of Gaea and Uranus, and they were hated by their father from the beginning. As soon as each one of them was born he would hide him away in the depths of the earth and would not allow him to return to the daylight.

Uranus delighted in his evil deed, but Gaea groaned within because she was filled with distress, and she planned an evil and deceitful trick. She quickly created gray steel, forged a great sickle, and explained her plan to her beloved sons. She spoke, encouraging them, but she was grieved at heart. "My children, offspring of a sinful father, if you have the will, we shall make your father pay for this wicked outrage, for he was the first to devise shameful acts." So she spoke, but terror seized them all, and not one of them uttered a sound. Great Cronus, however, took courage and spoke these words in answer to his beloved mother:

"Mother, I shall in truth take it upon myself to accomplish this deed, since I have no feeling for my father, who bears an evil name, for he plotted shameless deeds from the first." So he spoke, and Gaea was greatly delighted in her heart. She concealed him in an ambush and placed in his hands a sickle with sharp, jagged teeth and laid before him the whole plot.

Then mighty Uranus came, bringing the night with him, and he lay over Gaea with the longing of love, spreading out at full length, and his son stretched out his left hand from the ambush, grasping the huge jagged sickle in his right hand, and quickly cut the genitals from his father's body and cast them behind him.

They did not fall from his hands in vain, for Gaea received kindly all the drops of blood that fell from them. As time rolled on she bore the mighty Erinyes and the huge Giants, shining with armor, and the Nymphs, whom they call Meliae throughout the boundless earth.

As soon as Cronus cut off the organs with the steel and threw them from the land into the swelling sea, they were carried off on the surface of the water, and a white foam from the immortal flesh rose up around them, and within the foam a maiden came into being. First she was carried close to holy Cythera, and then from there she came to seagirt Cyprus. She stepped forth as a beautiful goddess, and all about her, grass grew up beneath her delicate feet. The gods and men call her Aphrodite, and also the foam-born goddess and fair-crowned Cytherea, because she arose from the foam near Cythera, and Cyprus-born, because she was born on wave-washed Cyprus.

And Eros [pictured as either her companion or son] walked beside her, and lovely Desire followed her from the first, when she was born and when she entered the assembly of the gods. She had this honor from the beginning, and this was the destiny allotted to her among men and the immortal gods—the conversations of young maidens, and smiles, deceptions and sweet delight, love and affection, and gentleness. [Led by Cronus, the Titans overthrow Uranus, and Cronus, the new leader of the gods, decides to marry his sister Rhea.] . . .

The Birth of Zeus

Rhea was joined in wedlock to Cronus and bore to him glorious children; Hestia, Demeter, Hera with sandals of gold, mighty

Hades, who dwells in his home below the earth and has a heart without pity, and loud-sounding Poseidon, the earth-shaker, and wise Zeus, the father of both gods and men, by whose thunder the broad earth is made to tremble.

Great Cronus swallowed these children as soon as each one came forth from his mother's womb, having this purpose in mind; that not any other one of the illustrious gods should have the honor of being king among the immortals. For he had learned from Gaea and starry Uranus that it was fated that even though he was powerful he would be overpowered by his own son, through the plans of mighty Zeus. For this reason he did not keep a blind watch, but lay in wait and swallowed each infant, while unceasing grief held Rhea in sorrow.

But when she was on the point of giving birth to Zeus, the father of gods and men, she turned in prayer to her dear parents, Gaea and starry Uranus, to contrive some plan with her so that she might bear the dear child without his knowledge, and that vengeance might be taken on the father for the children whom the mighty and crafty Cronus had swallowed. They in truth heard the plea of their beloved daughter and helped her, and they told her also what was fated to happen in regard to Cronus the king and his stout-hearted son.

Then they sent her to the fertile land of Crete, when she was about to give birth to the youngest of her children, great Zeus. Mighty Gaea took him willingly from her in broad Crete to nourish and rear. There Gaea carried him in her arms and hid him in a deep cave below the depths of the sacred earth on heavily wooded Mount Aegeum. She put into the arms of Cronus, the earlier king of the gods and the mighty son of Heaven, a great stone wrapped in swaddling clothes. Thereupon, lifting it up in his hands he put it down into his stomach, merciless as he was. He did not realize in his heart that his son, undefeated and carefree, had been left alive in place of the stone, and that his own son was soon destined to overpower him by an act of force and to keep him from his honors, reigning over the immortal gods himself.

As time rolled on, great Cronus, because he was tricked by the plans of Gaea, brought his offspring forth again, vomiting up first the stone he had swallowed last. Then Zeus set the stone firmly in the broad earth at sacred Pytho [an early name for Delphi] below the valleys of Parnassus, to be a sign from heaven from that time on, a thing of wonder to mortal men. He also freed from their bonds his father's brothers [the giants and monsters], the sons of Uranus, whom his father foolishly had bound fast. They remembered to show gratitude for his kindness and gave him thunder and the blazing thunderbolt and lightning. Trusting in these, he rules over mortals and immortals. . . .

As soon as their father, Uranus, became angry in his heart with [the monsters] Briareus and Cottus and Gyges, he bound

---

Rituals for Many Occasions

Religion pervaded nearly all aspects of ancient Greek life, as summarized here by noted Holy Cross College scholar Thomas R. Martin.

Greek religion encompassed many activities besides those of the cults of the twelve Olympian deities. Families marked important moments like birth, marriage, and death with prayers, sacrifices, and rituals. In the fifth century it became increasingly common for ordinary citizens, not just members of the elite, to make offerings at the tombs of their relatives. Nearly everyone consulted seers [psychics] about the meanings of dreams and omens and sought out magicians for spells to improve their love lives or curses to harm their enemies. Particularly important both to the community and to individuals were what we call hero cults, rituals performed at the tomb of a man or woman, usually from the distant past, whose remains were thought to retain special power. Athenian soldiers in the battle of Marathon in 490 B.C., for example, had reported having seen the ghost of the hero Theseus leading the way against the Persians. When Cimon in 475 B.C. brought back to Athens bones agreed to be those of Theseus, who was said to have died on a distant island, the people of Athens celebrated the occasion as a major triumph for their community and had the remains installed in a special shrine at the center of the city. The power of a hero's remains was local, whether for revealing the future through oracles, for healing injuries and disease, or for providing assistance in war. The only hero to whom cults were established internationally, all over the Greek world, was the strongman Heracles (Hercules). His superhuman feats in overcoming monsters and generally doing the impossible gave him an appeal as a protector in many city-states.

Thomas R. Martin, *Ancient Greece: From Prehistoric to Hellenistic Times.* New Haven, CT: Yale University Press, 1996, pp. 128–29.

them in strong bonds because he despised their arrogant manhood and their appearance and size, and he forced them to dwell below the broad-pathed earth at the edge of the world, grieving deeply for a long time and holding great sorrow in their hearts.

The War in Heaven

But the immortal gods whom fair-haired Rhea bore in wedlock to Cronus, at the bidding of Gaea, brought the three back again to the light; for she told them everything from beginning to end, explaining that with the three sons of Uranus they would win victory and a splendid achievement. For the Titan gods and those gods who were born of Cronus had been fighting a heartbreaking war for a long time. They struggled against each other in mighty combat, the illustrious Titans going into battle from lofty Othrys, while the gods whom fair-haired Rhea bore in wedlock to Cronus fought from Olympus.

Thus they held heartbreaking anger against each other and had been fighting without ceasing for ten long years. Nor was there any end to the bitter struggle, but the outcome of the war was hanging in the balance.

But when Zeus had furnished Briareus and Cottus and Gyges with all that was needed—nectar and ambrosia, the things that the very gods themselves eat—the manly spirit grew strong within the breasts of all three of them.

Then the father of both men and gods [Zeus] spoke to them: "Listen to me, splendid children of Gaea and Uranus, so that I may tell you what my heart bids me say. For the Titan gods and those who are born of Cronus have already been fighting for a very long time against each other to win a great victory. Now show your great power and invincible strength by opposing the Titans in fierce combat."

Thus he spoke, and blameless Cottus answered him: "Divine Zeus, you speak of things that are not unknown to us. It was because of your thoughtful planning that we came back again from the gloomy land of darkness and returned once more from cruel bondage, O king, son of Cronus. Now, therefore, with firm resolution and prudent planning we shall fight to defend your power in fierce combat, contending with the Titans in a violent struggle."

Thus he spoke, and the gods approved when they heard his

words, and their hearts longed for war even more than they had before. Then they all, both the females and the males, stirred up battle that day; the Titan gods and those who were born of Cronus, and also those mighty and powerful ones whom Zeus released from Erebus below the earth and brought back to the light. They had a hundred arms rising from their shoulders, and each had fifty heads growing out of his shoulders, set upon sturdy limbs.

These three indeed took their stand against the Titans in grim combat, holding enormous rocks in their powerful hands. The Titans, opposing them, quickly strengthened their ranks, and both sides at the same time displayed the mighty force of their hands. The boundless sea echoed and reechoed terribly, and the earth resounded loudly. The broad heaven groaned as it was shaken, and lofty Olympus [tallest peak in Greece] quivered on its foundations under the onslaught of the immortal gods. A heavy trembling reached dark Tartarus [a dark recess of the Underworld], as did the loud sound of their feet and their mighty weapons in the indescribable attack, when they hurled their dread missiles against each other. And the shouts of both sides rose to the starry heavens as they clashed with a great war cry.

Then Zeus no longer held his spirit in check; now his heart was filled with rage and he displayed all his power. He came from heaven and from Olympus hurling his lightning bolts without pause. The life-giving earth resounded all about with flames, and the great forest crackled on all sides with fire. All the earth throbbed with heat, and the streams of Oceanus and the barren sea were seething. The heat surrounded the earthbound Titans, and unspeakable flames reached up to the upper air, and the bright light of the flashing lightning took the sight from their eyes. A dreadful burning heat took possession of Chaos, and it seemed as if the earth and vast heaven above had come together, so great was the din as the gods opposed each other in strife. The terrible sound of fearful combat rose up, and acts of courage were displayed.

Until the end of the battle they faced each other and fought without ceasing in a fierce struggle. And among those in the front Cottus and Briareus and Gyges stirred up bitter fighting, for they hurled three hundred rocks from their sturdy hands, one after another, covered the Titans with their missiles, and sent them beneath the broad earth. Then, when they had overpowered them by force, even though they [the Titans] were full of spirit, they bound them in heavy chains as far down below the earth as heaven is above the earth—for that is the distance from earth to dark Tartarus. A bronze anvil falling for nine nights and nine days from heaven would reach the earth on the tenth, and, in turn, a bronze anvil falling for nine nights and nine days from earth would reach Tartarus on the tenth.

Dark and Murky Tartarus

Around Tartarus stretches a wall of bronze, and night spreads about it in three rows, and, moreover, above it grow the roots of the earth and of the barren sea. In that place the Titan gods have been hidden by the plan of Zeus the cloud-gatherer under the gloomy darkness in a dank region at the extreme edge of the vast earth. There is no way out for them, for Poseidon placed on it gates of bronze, and a wall surrounds it on all sides. There Gyges and Cottus and great-hearted Briareus dwell, the faithful guardians of aegis-bearing Zeus. [The aegis was a sturdy protective shield or breastplate associated with Zeus and Athena.]

And there in order are the sources and ends of the dark earth and murky Tartarus and the barren sea and starry heaven, all dreadfully dark and dank, hated even by the gods. There the terrible home of dark Night stands covered over with murky clouds. Standing in front of this, Atlas, the son of Iapetus, holds up the wide heaven on his head and untiring hands without moving, where Night and Day come quite close, addressing each other in greeting as they cross the great bronze threshold. While one is coming down inside and the other is going out through the door, the house does not keep them both inside at the same time. But one is always outside the house and moves over the earth while the other is, in turn, inside the house and waits until the hour of her own journey arrives. One holds full-seeing light for men on earth, while the other, deadly Night, covered by a murky cloud, holds in her arms Sleep, the brother of Death.

There also the children of black Night have their homes; Sleep and Death, terrible gods. Never does the shining Sun look upon them with his rays, either as he goes forth into heaven or as he returns from heaven. Of these, the former, Sleep, lingers over the earth and the broad surface of the sea and is gentle and kind to men, but the other has a heart of iron, and the spirit of bronze within his breast is pitiless, and he holds fast to whatever man he has seized and is hated even by the immortal gods.

There, in the front, the echoing chambers of the god of the lower world, mighty Hades, and his wife, dread Persephone, stand, and a terrible dog guards the entrance; a dog without pity, and he has an evil habit. He welcomes those who enter with his tail wagging and his ears erect, but does not allow anyone to go out again, for he lies in wait and chews up whomever he finds leaving the gates.

And in that place dwells the goddess hated by the immortal gods, dread Styx, the eldest daughter of Oceanus, who [as a dark river] flows back into himself. She dwells apart from the gods in a splendid house overarched with huge rocks and supported all around by silver columns reaching toward heaven. Seldom does swift-footed Iris come to her with a message over the wide surface of the sea. When discord and strife appear among the immortal gods, however, and when any one of those who dwell on Olympus has spoken falsely, then Zeus sends Iris to bring the mighty oath of the gods from afar in a golden pitcher, the renowned chill water that runs down from a steep and lofty rock. . . .

And there in order are the sources and ends of the dark earth, and murky Tartarus and the barren sea and starry heaven, all dreadfully dark and dank, hated even by the gods. There, also, are gleaming entrance gates and an immovable threshold of bronze. And over this threshold and apart from all the gods the Titans live, on the other side of gloomy Chaos. But the splendid allies of loud-thundering Zeus—Cottus and Gyges—dwell in homes on the bottom of Oceanus. And, indeed, since Briareus was brave, Poseidon the heavy-sounding earth-shaker made him his son-in-law and gave him his daughter in marriage.

An Athenian on Trial for Murder

Lysias

The following court speech (translated by Kathleen Freeman) was written at Athens sometime between 400 and 380 B.C. by Lysias (ca.459–ca.380), a renowned orator and speechwriter (*logographos*). His client was the defendant in the case, one Euphiletus, who had been accused of murder. The circumstances were that Euphiletus's wife had been seduced by a man named Eratosthenes and Euphiletus had caught the adulterers in bed and slain Eratosthenes on the spot. According to Athenian law, a husband was allowed to slay his wife's lover as long as adultery was the sole reason for the act. If the slayer had some other motive for the killing, he could be prosecuted for murder; and this was how Euphiletus ended up in court. Eratosthenes' relatives accused him of arranging the meeting between his wife and Eratosthenes as part of a preconceived murder plan. Euphiletus insisted that this was a lie and that he had merely availed himself of the law as written.

Note the skill with which Lysias structures the defense, creating a careful, detailed picture of a kindhearted, trusting husband who is deceived by his wife and her disreputable lover. The speech also suggests to the jurors that in acquitting Euphiletus they will be sending a message to other would-be home wreckers and thereby doing the community a service. The various sections of the speech, including the Proem (introduction), Narrative, Arguments, and Epilogue (conclusion), are standard elements of the formal rhetoric (art of persuasive speech) that the Greeks developed and the Romans adopted and perpetuated. The verdict in this case is unknown, but it is likely that Euphiletus was acquitted, for adultery was considered a serious offense among the Greeks.

Lysias, "On the Killing of Eratosthenes the Seducer," *The Murder of Herodes and Other Trials from the Athenian Law Courts,* edited by Kathleen Freeman. New York: W.W. Norton, 1963.

The Proem

I would give a great deal, members of the jury, to find you, as judges of this case, taking the same attitude towards me as you would adopt towards your own behaviour in similar circumstances. I am sure that if you felt about others in the same way as you did about yourselves, not one of you would fail to be angered by these deeds, and all of you would consider the punishment a small one for those guilty of such conduct.

Moreover, the same opinion would be found prevailing not only among you, but everywhere throughout Greece. This is the one crime for which, under any government, democratic or exclusive, equal satisfaction is granted to the meanest against the mightiest, so that the least of them receives the same justice as the most exalted. Such is the detestation, members of the jury, in which this outrage is held by all mankind.

Concerning the severity of the penalty, therefore, you are, I imagine, all of the same opinion: not one of you is so easy-going as to believe that those guilty of such great offences should obtain pardon, or are deserving of a light penalty. What I have to prove, I take it, is just this: that Eratosthenes seduced my wife, and that in corrupting her he brought shame upon my children and outrage upon me, by entering my home; that there was no other enmity between him and me except this; and that I did not commit this act for the sake of money, in order to rise from poverty to wealth, nor for any other advantage except the satisfaction allowed by law.

I shall expound my case to you in full from the beginning, omitting nothing and telling the truth. In this alone lies my salvation, I imagine—if I can explain to you everything that happened.

The Narrative

Members of the jury: when I decided to marry and had brought a wife home, at first my attitude towards her was this: I did not wish to annoy her, but neither was she to have too much of her own way. I watched her as well as I could, and kept an eye on her as was proper. But later, after my child had been born, I came to trust her, and I handed all my possessions over to her, believing that this was the greatest possible proof of affection.

Well, members of the jury, in the beginning she was the best of women. She was a clever housewife, economical and exact in her management of everything. But then, my mother died; and her death has proved to be the source of all my troubles, because it was when my wife went to the funeral that this man Eratosthenes saw her; and as time went on, he was able to seduce her. He kept a look out for our maid who goes to market; and approaching her with his suggestions, he succeeded in corrupting her mistress.

Now first of all, gentlemen, I must explain that I have a small house which is divided into two—the men's quarters and the women's—each having the same space, the women upstairs and the men downstairs.

After the birth of my child, his mother nursed him; but I did not want her to run the risk of going downstairs every time she had to give him a bath, so I myself took over the upper storey, and let the women have the ground floor. And so it came about that by this time it was quite customary for my wife often to go downstairs and sleep with the child, so that she could give him the breast and stop him from crying.

This went on for a long while, and I had not the slightest suspicion. On the contrary, I was in such a fool's paradise that I believed my wife to be the chastest woman in all the city.

Time passed, gentlemen. One day, when I had come home unexpectedly from the country, after dinner, the child began crying and complaining. Actually it was the maid who was pinching him on purpose to make him behave so, because—as I found out later—this man was in the house.

Well, I told my wife to go and feed the child, to stop his crying. But at first she refused, pretending that she was so glad to see me back after my long absence. At last I began to get annoyed, and I insisted on her going.

"Oh, yes!" she said. "To leave *you* alone with the maid up here! You mauled her about before, when you were drunk!"

I laughed. She got up, went out, closed the door—pretending that it was a joke—and locked it. As for me, I thought no harm of all this, and I had not the slightest suspicion. I went to sleep, glad to do so after my journey from the country.

Towards morning, she returned and unlocked the door.

I asked her why the doors had been creaking during the night.

She explained that the lamp beside the baby had gone out, and that she had then gone to get a light from the neighbours.

I said no more. I thought it really was so. But it did seem to me, members of the jury, that she had done up her face with cosmetics, in spite of the fact that her brother had died only a month before. Still, even so, I said nothing about it. I just went off, without a word.

After this, members of the jury, an interval elapsed, during which my injuries had progressed, leaving me far behind. Then, one day, I was approached by an old hag. She had been sent by a woman—Eratosthenes' previous mistress, as I found out later. This woman, furious because he no longer came to see her as before, had been on the look-out until she had discovered the reason. The old crone, therefore, had come and was lying in wait for me near my house.

"Euphiletus," she said, "please don't think that my approaching you is in any way due to a wish to interfere. The fact is, the man who is wronging you and your wife is an enemy of ours. Now if you catch the woman who does your shopping and works for you, and put her through an examination, you will discover all. The culprit," she added, "is Eratosthenes from Oea. Your wife is not the only one he has seduced—there are plenty of others. It's his profession."

With these words, members of the jury, she went off.

At once I was overwhelmed. Everything rushed into my mind, and I was filled with suspicion. I reflected how I had been locked into the bedroom. I remembered how on that night the middle and outer doors had creaked, a thing that had never happened before; and how I had had the idea that my wife's face was rouged. All these things rushed into my mind, and I was filled with suspicion.

I went back home, and told the servant to come with me to market. I took her instead to the house of one of my friends; and there I informed her that I had discovered all that was going on in my house.

"As for you," I said, "two courses are open to you: either to be flogged and sent to the tread-mill, and never be released from a life of utter misery; or to confess the whole truth and suffer no punishment, but win pardon from me for your wrong-doing. Tell me no lies. Speak the whole truth."

At first she tried denial, and told me that I could do as I pleased—she knew nothing. But when I named Eratosthenes to her face, and said that he was the man who had been visiting my wife, she was dumbfounded, thinking that I had found out everything exactly. And then at last, falling at my feet and exacting a promise from me that no harm should be done to her, she denounced the villain. She described how he had first approached her after the funeral, and then how in the end she had passed the message on, and in course of time my wife had been overpersuaded. She explained the way in which he had contrived to get into the house, and how when I was in the country my wife had gone to a religious service with this man's mother, and everything else that had happened. She recounted it all exactly.

When she had told all, I said:

"See to it that nobody gets to know of this; otherwise the promise I made you will not hold good. And furthermore, I expect you to show me this actually happening. I have no use for words. I want the *fact* to be exhibited, if it really is so."

She agreed to do this.

Four or five days then elapsed, as I shall prove to you by important evidence. But before I do so, I wish to narrate the events of the last day.

I had a friend and relative named Sôstratus. He was coming home from the country after sunset when I met him. I knew that as he had got back so late, he would not find any of his own people at home; so I asked him to dine with me. We went home to my place, and going upstairs to the upper storey, we had dinner there. When he felt restored, he went off; and I went to bed.

Then, members of the jury, Eratosthenes made his entry; and the maid wakened me and told me that he was in the house.

I told her to watch the door; and going downstairs, I slipped out noiselessly.

I went to the houses of one man after another. Some I found at home; others, I was told, were out of town. So collecting as many as I could of those who were there, I went back. We procured torches from the shop near by, and entered my house. The door had been left open by arrangement with the maid.

We forced the bedroom door. The first of us to enter saw him still lying beside my wife. Those who followed saw him standing naked on the bed.

I knocked him down, members of the jury, with one blow. I then twisted his hands behind his back and tied them. And then I asked him why he was committing this crime against me, of breaking into my house.

He answered that he admitted his guilt; but he begged and besought me not to kill him—to accept a money-payment instead.

But I replied:

"It is not I who shall be killing you, but the law of the State, which you, in transgressing, have valued less highly than your own pleasures. You have preferred to commit this great crime against my wife and my children, rather than to obey the law and be of decent behaviour."

Thus, members of the jury, this man met the fate which the laws prescribe for wrong-doers of his kind.

The Arguments

Eratosthenes was not seized in the street and carried off, nor had he taken refuge at the altar, as the prosecution alleges. The facts do not admit of it: he was struck in the bedroom, he fell at once, and I bound his hands behind his back. There were so many present that he could not possibly escape through their midst, since he had neither steel nor wood nor any other weapon with which he could have defended himself against all those who had entered the room.

No, members of the jury: you know as well as I do how wrong-doers will not admit that their adversaries are speaking the truth, and attempt by lies and trickery of other kinds to excite the anger of the hearers against those whose acts are in accordance with Justice.

(*To the Clerk of the Court*):

Read the Law.

(*The Law of Solon is read, that an adulterer may be put to death by the man who catches him.*)

He made no denial, members of the jury. He admitted his guilt, and begged and implored that he should not be put to death, offering to pay compensation. But I would not accept his estimate. I preferred to accord a higher authority to the law of the State, and I took that satisfaction which you, because you thought it the most just, have decreed for those who commit such offences.

Witnesses to the preceding, kindly step up.

(*The witnesses come to the front of the Court, and the Clerk reads their depositions. When the Clerk has finished reading, and the witnesses have agreed that the depositions are correct, the defendant again addresses the Clerk*):

Now please read this further law from the pillar of the Court of the Areopagus:

(*The Clerk reads another version of Solon's law, as recorded on the pillar of the Areopagus Court.*)

You hear, members of the jury, how it is expressly decreed by the Court of the Areopagus itself, which both traditionally and in your own day has been granted the right to try cases of murder, that no person shall be found guilty of murder who catches an adulterer with his wife and inflicts this punishment. The Lawgiver was so strongly convinced of the justice of these provisions in the case of married women, that he applied them also to concubines, who are of less importance. Yet obviously, if he had known of any greater punishment than this for cases where married women are concerned, he would have provided it. But in fact, as it was impossible for him to invent any more severe penalty for corruption of wives, he decided to provide the same punishment as in the case of concubines.

(*To the Clerk of the Court*):

Please read me this Law also.

(*The Clerk reads out further clauses from Solon's laws on rape.*)

You hear, members of the jury, how the Lawgiver ordains that if anyone debauch by force a free man or boy, the fine shall be double that decreed in the case of a slave. If anyone debauch a woman—in which case it is *permitted* to kill him—he shall be liable to the same fine. Thus, members of the jury, the Lawgiver considered violators deserving of a lesser penalty than seducers: for the latter he provided the death-penalty; for the former, the doubled fine. His idea was that those who use force are loathed by the persons violated, whereas those who have got their way by persuasion corrupt women's minds, in such a way as to make other men's wives more attached to themselves than to their husbands, so that the whole house is in their power, and it is uncertain who is the children's father, the husband or the lover. These considerations caused the Lawgiver to affix death as the penalty for seduction. . . .

You have heard the witnesses, members of the jury. Now consider the case further in your own minds, inquiring whether there had ever existed between Eratosthenes and myself any other enmity but this. You will find none. He never brought any malicious charge against me, nor tried to secure my banishment, nor prosecuted me in any private suit. Neither had he knowledge of any crime of which I feared the revelation, so that I desired to kill him; nor by carrying out this act did I hope to gain money. So far from ever having had any dispute with him, or drunken brawl, or any other quarrel, I had never even set eyes on the man before that night. What possible object could I have had, therefore, in running so great a risk, except that I had suffered the greatest of all injuries at his hands? Again, would I myself have called in witnesses to my crime, when it was possible for me, if I desired to murder him without justification, to have had no confidants?

The Epilogue

It is my belief, members of the jury, that this punishment was inflicted not in my own interests, but in those of the whole community. Such villains, seeing the rewards which await their crimes, will be less ready to commit offences against others if they see that you too hold the same opinion of them. Otherwise it would be far better to wipe out the existing laws and make different ones, which will penalise those who keep guard over their own wives, and grant full immunity to those who criminally pursue them. This would be a far more just procedure than to set a trap for citizens by means of the laws, which urge the man who catches an adulterer to do with him whatever he will, and yet allow the injured party to undergo a trial far more perilous than that which faces the law-breaker who seduces other men's wives. Of this, I am an example—I, who now stand in danger of losing life, property, everything, because I have obeyed the laws of the State.

The Athenian Assembly

Donald Kagan

Of all the democratic institutions created in ancient Athens, the *Ekklesia*, or Assembly, a meeting of all the citizens, was the most fundamental and powerful. From the authority vested in and exercised by the majority of citizens flowed the laws and policies of the state. The most important way that Athens's Assembly differed from the legislatures of modern democracies was that it was direct and pure rather indirect and representational. Individual, everyday people of all walks of life, not their elected representatives, met and decided their own fate. Yale University's Donald Kagan, a noted authority on ancient Athenian democracy, provides this overview of how the members of the Athenian Assembly met and conducted their business. He highlights his brisk narrative with excerpts from two plays by the fifth-century B.C. comic playwright Aristophanes (one of which pokes fun at Aristophanes' colleague, the tragedian Euripides) and a speech by the great fourth-century B.C. Athenian orator Demosthenes.

A t the heart of what we would call the legislative branch of the Athenian democracy was the assembly (*ekklesia*). It was open to all adult male citizens of Athens, during Pericles' lifetime perhaps as many as forty thousand men. Most Athenians lived many miles from the city and few owned horses, so attendance required a long walk to town. As a result, the number taking part was probably from five to six thousand, although some actions required a quorum of six thousand. The meetings took place on a hill called the Pnyx, not far from the Acropolis and overlooking the Agora. The citizens sat on the earth of the sharply sloping hill, and the speakers stood on a low platform. It was not easy for them to make themselves heard; Demosthenes, the great fourth-century orator, is said to have practiced speaking by the

Donald Kagan, *Pericles of Athens and the Birth of Democracy*. New York: Free Press, 1991. Copyright © 1991 by Donald Kagan. Reproduced by permission of the publisher.

seashore over the crashing surf to make his voice strong enough for his work on the Pnyx.

We can get some idea of the opening of these meetings from a comic version in Aristophanes' *Acharnians*, performed in 425. The first speaker is a typical Aristophanic comic hero, an old-fashioned farmer who complains about the war because it keeps him in Athens, away from his farm in the country:

> It is the day of an assembly and already morning, but the Pnyx is deserted. They are chattering in the Agora, dodging the rope dripping with red dye. [A squad of slaves roamed the streets and swatted obvious shirkers with such ropes, leaving red marks on their tunics. Anyone caught with such stains had to pay a fine.] Even the Presidents of the Assembly have not arrived. They will be late, and when they finally come they will push and fight each other for a seat in the front row, streaming down all together, you can't imagine how; but they will say nothing about making peace. Oh my Athens! I am always the first to make the return voyage to the assembly and take my seat. And since I am alone, I groan, I yawn, I stretch my legs, I fart, I don't know what to do, I write, pull out my loose hairs, add up my accounts, looking off at my fields, longing for peace, hating the town, sick for my village-home, which never said "buy my charcoal, my vinegar, my oil"; the word "buy" is unknown there where everything is free. And so, I have come here fully prepared to shout, to interrupt and abuse the speakers if they talk about anything but peace. But here come these noontime Presidents. Didn't I tell you? Didn't I predict how they would come? Everyone jostling for the front seat!

Next, the herald of the assembly says, "Move up! Move up within the consecrated area!" Then he recites the formula that regularly began debate in the assembly: "Who wishes to speak?"

Opening Prayers and Curses

The scene in *Acharnians* omits the prayer that began sessions of the assembly and preceded the beginning of business. We can get an idea of what that was like from the parody Aristophanes presents in another of his comedies, the *Thesmophoriazusae*. The humor in the passage derives from the hilarious idea of women holding a political assembly and from Euripides' reputation as a misogynist. The herald recites the opening prayer, which included a curse on those who would subvert the democratic constitition:

Let there be silence, let there be silence. Pray to the Thes-
mophorae, Demeter and Kore, and to Plutus and Calligeneia and
to Earth the foster mother, and to Hermes and the Graces that this
present assembly and meeting may do what is finest and best,

An Old-Fashioned
Athenian Criticizes Democracy

*Although most Athenians were happy with and proud of their democracy,
a few old-fashioned types were not. One was an anonymous citizen that
modern scholars call the "Old Oligarch," who left behind a scathing criticism of democratic government, excerpted here. His main gripe is that the
system sacrifices the needs and rights of the "better," "cleverer" classes in
favor of those of the "baser," "ignorant" commoners.*

Now, as for the [democratic] constitution of the Athenians . . . I
praise it not, in so far as the very choice involves the welfare of the
baser folk as opposed to that of the better class. . . . In fact, all the
world over, the cream of society is in opposition to the democracy.
Naturally, [this is because] the smallest amount of intemperance
and injustice, together with the highest scrupulousness in the pur-
suit of excellence, is to be found in the ranks of the better class,
while within the ranks of the People will be found the greatest
amount of ignorance. . . . It was a mistake to allow [the members
of the lower classes] the universal right of speech and a seat in
council. These should have been reserved for the cleverest, the
flower of the community. . . . Now, anyone who likes, any base
fellow, may get up and discover something [such as a law, regula-
tion, or policy] to the advantage of himself and his equals. . . . The
ignorance and the baseness of this fellow, together with his goodwill, are worth a great deal more to [the commoners] than your
superior person's virtue and wisdom. . . . A state founded upon
such institutions will not be the best state. . . . If you seek for good
legislation, in the first place you will see the cleverest members of
the community laying down the laws for the rest. . . . Another
point is the extraordinary amount of license granted to slaves and
resident aliens at Athens, where a blow [delivered to a slave] is il-
legal, and a slave will not step aside to let you pass him in the
street. . . . [Even worse] an Athenian might be mistaken for a slave
or an alien and receive a beating; since the Athenian [common-
ers] are not better clothed than the slave or alien, nor in personal
appearance is there any superiority.

Quoted in *Constitution of the Athenians*, trans. H.G. Dakyns, in C.A. Robinson, *Athens
in the Age of Pericles.* Norman: University of Oklahoma, 1971, pp. 21–26.

bringing advantage and good fortune both to Athens and to ourselves. And let the woman who acts and speaks best for the Athenian people and for Womankind win out. Pray for this and for good things for yourselves. Io Paean! Io Paean! Let us rejoice.

The assembly of women responds with a choral song of prayer. Then the herald recites the curse:

> Pray to the Olympian and Pythian and Delian gods and goddesses, and to the other gods that if anyone plots evil against the people of Womankind or is negotiating with Euripides or the Persians to the harm of the people of Womankind, or aims at becoming a tyrant or at restoring a tyrant, or denounces a woman for palming off someone else's baby as her own, or if there is a slave who is an accomplice in her mistress' intrigues and betrays her secret to her master, or who does not deliver messages faithfully, or if there is a lover who gets what he wants from a woman with lies but never carries out his promises . . . may he and his family die a horrible death; and pray that the gods give many good things to all the rest of you women.

Again the chorus responds with a prayerful song. Then the herald turns to business:

> Listen all! Approved by the Council of Women, moved by Sostrata, Timoclea was president and Lysilla secretary; to hold an assembly on the middle day of the Festival of Thesmorphoria in the morning, when we all have most leisure; the first item on the agenda will be: what should be done with Euripides, since it is clear that he wrongs us all? Who wishes to speak?

If we put aside the jokes at the expense of women, substitute "the people of Athens" for "the people of Womankind," and add "those who bring false reports and those who deceive the people" to the list of those accursed we will be left with a fair approximation of the form in which the assembly began its business.

All Power to the People

But the real meetings on the Pnyx were rarely comic; they dealt with serious questions. The assembly had four fixed meetings in each of the ten periods into which the official year was divided, and special meetings were called when needed. Topics included approval or disapproval of treaties and making declarations of war, assigning generals to campaigns and deciding what forces and resources they should command, confirmation of officials or their removal from office, whether or not to hold an ostracism, questions concerning religion, questions of inheritance, and, in fact, everything else. In the second meeting of each period "anyone who wishes can address the people on whatever subject he likes, whether private or public," and the third and fourth meetings discussed "all other kinds of business," whatever that might be.

It is especially impressive for a citizen of a modern representative democracy to read of these great town meetings dealing directly with questions of foreign policy—questions that could mean life or death for those present at the debate and for their city. Many such dramatic assemblies met in Pericles' time, but the one best described took place almost a century after his death. Philip of Macedon had marched into central Greece, only three days' march from Athens, one of his greatest enemies. What to do, whether to resist or try to negotiate such terms as they could, these decisions could determine the fate of Athens and its people, and they would be decided on the Pnyx by the assembled masses. Demosthenes, leader of the resistance to Philip, gives his version of the meeting.

> It was evening when a messenger came to the presidents of the Council to report that Elatea had been taken. In the midst of their dinner they got up at once and cleared the booths in the marketplace . . . while others sent for the generals and called for the trumpeter, and the city was filled with commotion. At dawn on the next day the presidents called the Council to the Council House, and you [the Athenian people] went to the assembly, and before the Council began proceedings and made any proposal the whole people was seated up on the Pynx. Then the Council arrived, the presidents reported the news it had received and introduced the messenger who had brought it. When he had spoken the herald asked, "Who wishes to speak?" And no one came forward. (from *On the Crown*)

To get an idea of the distance between ancient and modern democracy we need only consider how an emergency—like the seizure of an American embassy—would be dealt with today in the United States. It would probably arrive first as secret information at some bureau of the government's vast and complex intelligence service. It would be treated as highly confidential and revealed only to a few people in the White House and the State and Defense departments. Policy would be discussed in a small, closed group, and the decision made by one man, the president. If there were no leaks, the people would hear of it only when the die had been cast.

Questions no less grave than the one confronting the Athenians of Demosthenes' time arose more than once in Periclean Athens. Each time, the popular assembly held a full debate and made the decision by raising their hands in a vote determined by a simple majority. There can be no stronger evidence of the full and final sovereignty of the Athenian people.

Banking and Local Industries

W.G. Hardy

This well-written summary of ancient Greek financial affairs is by former University of Alberta scholar W.G. Hardy. Because most of the surviving evidence comes from Athens, his discussion focuses on the local industries and money matters of that city-state, which was the largest and most prosperous in Greece. Covered are the local artisans who manufactured various goods in small shops, which frequently doubled as their homes. Then he describes the retail sellers (middlemen), who were mostly *metics* (foreigners living in Athens), the bankers and traders, and also the well-to-do local citizens who helped the community function by providing it with financial support.

U ntil the Peloponnesian War, many Athenians were still on the farm and many city-dwellers held property in the country. . . .

Yet Periclean Athens was, after all, one of the major trading-centres of the Mediterranean. This pre-eminence was won and maintained by bankers, wholesale traders, and merchant-skippers, but above all by her craftsmen.

Small Shopkeepers

Today, north of the Acropolis, there is a narrow street called Shoe Lane. If you walk down it, on both sides of you are shoes and boots and still more boots and shoes. Shoe Lane is a sort of vestigial reminder of industry in ancient Athens. There were shoemakers, metal-workers, dyers, tanners, jewellers, stonemasons, and a host of other craftsmen. But instead of mass-production in huge factories crammed with machinery, Athenian shoes, pots, sausages, hoes, axes, and the like were turned out by workers in small shops. These shops were often both the plants for manufacturing the goods, and the outlets for selling them. Often, as in much of the Near East today, they were also the homes of the

W.G. Hardy, *The Greek and Roman World*. Cambridge, MA: Schenkman, 1962. Copyright © 1962 by W.G. Hardy. Reproduced by permission of the publisher.

craftsmen. Most of these small plants were run by a man and his apprentices, aided by a slave or two. To make the situation still more confusing from a North American point of view, all the workers of one craft lived side by side. The potters of Athens, for instance, all crowded together in the Cerameicus. . . .

If you will allow your imagination to roam for a moment, you can hear the hammers of the sweating metal-workers ring and see their forges glowing; or you can stroll through a narrow street in the Cerameicus and watch a potter moulding a lump of clay on his spinning wheel or a vase-painter drawing a design. It may be a picture of Achilles killing Hector or of men dicing or of a riot of Maenads and Sileni. But there is one important point to remember. Those vases piled around you, about the artistry of which we rave today, were manufactured not for showpieces but for sale in one of the most fiercely competitive markets of the ancient world. Attic pots had to be good pots. Their beauty of form and design is incidental, though not accidental. They were made by craftsmen who took pride in their handiwork.

In addition to direct sales from producer to consumer, there were a swarm of retail traders, called *kapeloi*. They were to be found in the stalls of the Agora, or market-place, or in the shops round about. We read of confectioners, slave-dealers, fishmongers, vintners, and the like, and of pedlars who carried goods out through the countryside. To the Greek, however, a middleman was always faintly suspect as a parasite on the body public. Thus, Aristotle says of retail trade in his *Politics* that it is a 'kind of exchange which is justly censured; for it is unnatural and a mode by which men gain from one another'.

Most of the retail traders were *metics*, that is, resident aliens. The craftsmen were a mixture of *metics*, slaves, and Athenian citizens. In their hands, then, was the bulk of the production and much of the retail trade in Athens. We ought to note that there was a special 'potters' market'.

Such craftsmen-cum-shopkeepers were not, so to speak, tied to a time-clock or to punching a single button on an assembly-line. They were freemen who took time off whenever they liked. Socrates, the teacher and inspiration of the philosopher Plato, was a stonemason. Yet in the Platonic dialogues we find him in the gymnasia or in the streets or at the festivals or at dinners, continually questioning the people he met in an insatiable search for truth. There was only one Socrates. Yet it is clear that his fellow-craftsmen were, on the whole, more interested, as long as they could make a simple living, in recreation or in politics or in discussion or in a stroll with a friend, than in piling up possessions. Yet these were the men who executed the perfect and intricate workmanship of the Parthenon, the Hephaesteion . . . and the Erechtheum [three famous Athenian temples]. . . .

For the building of such imperishable monuments as the Parthenon, which took nine years to complete, the State hired quarrymen, transport-workers, carpenters, masons, goldsmiths, and sculptors. Sometimes a piece of work was let out on contract. At other times the men were paid directly by the State. Sculptors got the same wage as masons. So did slaves.

The whole picture of basic Athenian industry, except for the

The Lucrative Grain-Shipping Business

In this excerpt from his classic book, The Ancient Mariners, *noted scholar Lionel Casson tells about the most lucrative form of trade in the Greek world—exporting and importing grain.*

Far and away the biggest business in Athens was the importing of grain. The ancient Greek lived principally off bread and porridge; if supplies weren't unloaded regularly on the quays of the Peiraeus [the port of Athens], the populace faced hardship. The same was true of most of the larger Greek cities. Intense commercial competition took place in this age, with many a clash of interests; it was not over markets in which to sell surplus products but over access to supplies essential for keeping a city going: grain for food, wine to drink, and olive oil which, by itself, did in those days what soap and butter and electricity do for us. Athens grew olives; wine could be got nearby; but the most important, grain, was available in quantity in only three places, all of them far overseas: Egypt, Sicily, and South Russia. In the Peloponnesian War Sparta starved Athens into submission by destroying her fleet and blockading her port; a little over half a century later King Philip of Macedon, the able father of Alexander the Great, went about achieving the same result by occupying the city of Byzantium and closing the gates of the Bosporus, thereby cutting access to South Russian grain. . . .

It usually took four men of business, each playing a specific role, to bring a cargo from the wheatfields of South Russia or Egypt or silver mines, implies a different set of values from our own. The craftsmen knew their trade, whatever it was, though their tools were of the simplest. Yet, in general, they seem to have preferred a full participation in the life of the city to being tied too long to any manual occupation or to getting ahead financially. From the Erechtheum inscriptions of 409 B.C. we know that the usual rate of pay was a drachma a day. . . . From other references in Greek authors it can be estimated that it cost a single man about 120 drachmai a year . . . to live, and a married man with two children double that amount.

The major point, though, is that the Athenian workmen could, and apparently did, have plenty of leisure time. It would take a single man only a little more than two days of work a week to earn a living.

In passing, it ought to be mentioned that there were a few

Sicily to the miller at Athens: shipper, shipowner, banker, and wholesaler; in many cases it took a pair or group of partners to provide the capital for each of the roles. The shipper practically always worked on credit and generally with a chartered vessel. He contracted with a shipowner for a ship or space on one and then borrowed money from some banker . . . to pay for the freight charges and a load of merchandise. Those who owned their own ships pledged them as security, but most put up the cargo they intended to buy. Obviously they must have been by and large men of integrity, for the banker never saw his security until months after the loan was made, when the vessel with its load finally docked at the Peiraeus. Interest for this service ran high, 22½ to 30 per cent for the four to five months of the sailing season, that is, between 67½ and 90 per cent per annum; but that was only natural. There was no insurance in those days; the banker assumed total responsibility—if the vessel failed to come back he, not the shipper, lost everything—so his reward had to be big enough to compensate for all risks. And these were considerable because, alongside the purely maritime ones, there was the ever present possibility of seizure by hostile men-of-war or attack by pirates. The same risks plus the lack of any system of insurance made the shippers and shipowners anxious to work as much as they could with borrowed funds even when they had some of their own; in this way they limited their personal loss when a venture ran into trouble.

Lionel Casson, *The Ancient Mariners.* New York: Macmillan, 1959, pp. 113–14.

cases of mass-manufacturing. In Plato's *Republic* the discussions are supposed to take place in the Peiraeus at the home of Cephalus, a rich *metic*. Cephalus, we learn, manufactured shields and employed, apparently, 120 men. Moreover, the silver mines at Laureion were let out by the State to individuals who worked them by means of slaves. Nicias, the rich man and general who, more than any other single individual, was responsible for the disaster which befell the Athenians in Sicily, is said to have rented out a thousand slaves to the silver mines.

Apart from these few instances, the craftsmen of Athens supplied most of the home market. In the case of the potters, they also furnished an important article for export. Pottery was the dinnerware of the ancient world; but it was also used for storing every kind of liquid and dry goods—and pottery was always getting broken. So there was a fierce competition between Corinth and Athens for the pottery market of the Mediterranean. In the fifth century B.C., Attic red-figured vases won the battle.

For its export trade which, in addition to pottery, consisted chiefly of the export of olive-oil, wine, figs, and armour, Athens needed bankers, wholesale traders, and merchant-skippers. Most of these were *metics*.

Sparta periodically expelled all foreigners within her boundaries. Athens, under Pericles, encouraged strangers to settle. *Metics* could not vote or hold office and had to be represented in the law-courts by an Athenian. Yet they paid taxes which included a special head-tax per family of 12 drachmai. . . . They were selected for liturgies, about which more will be said, and served in the army and navy. Like the Athenian citizens, they seem to have been proud of the city, and they were of tremendous assistance to banking and foreign trade.

The primary function of the bankers, or tablemen as they were called, was to change coins. By Periclean days, they were also well advanced in taking in money on deposit and in making loans. Pasion, the famous fourth-century B.C. banker, began life as a slave to a banker. Then he married his master's widow and took over the bank. At his death his assets were fifty talents [300,000 drachmai]. . . . Of this amount eleven talents, or somewhat more than a fifth, were on deposit.

The minimum interest rate was twelve per cent. On loans on

ships or on ships' cargoes the rate ran up to twenty or thirty per cent; this because of a provision that if a ship was lost at sea or captured by pirates the loan was cancelled. Aristotle, again, has hard words for the banker. 'The most hated sort [of moneymaking] and with the greatest reason,' he writes, 'is usury, which makes a gain out of money itself. . . . For money was intended to be used in exchange, but not to increase at interest.'

Without the banker the wholesale trader or *emporos* would have found it difficult to operate. The method of the *emporos* was to buy a large consignment of goods and to hire space on a ship for it to be taken from city to city in search of a market. If successful, the wholesale trader would come to own his own ship and would become a merchant-skipper or *naukleros*. No sailing was done in winter. But each spring the merchant-skippers would load their round-bellied tubs—a Greek merchantman could carry only about 7,000 bushels of wheat—with olive-oil and wine in Attic jars and with the finest of Attic vases. Shields, spears, and helmets might be part of the cargo. So might jars filled with beads, necklaces, and other trinkets—this for trade with backward people.

Then the skipper would set out for a season's adventuring from port to port. He might, for example, unload at Massalia, now Marseilles, and take on hides and cheese, trade these at Carthage for rugs and cushions, exchange these at Naucratis in Egypt for ivory, papyrus, and linen, and so on. Or he might move into the Black Sea to bring back, finally, a cargo of wheat. Meanwhile, that same spring, other ships would be setting out from Miletus, Syracuse, Cyrene, Corinth, Carthage, and the other Mediterranean ports, with the same sort of trading venture in mind. Everywhere there would be warehouses in which the merchants could display their goods. Everywhere they would have to pay customs dues—at Athens these were two per cent on all exports and imports—and harbour tolls.

It was in this somewhat hit-or-miss but adventurous fashion that the trade of the ancient world was carried on. By this method the products of all known countries flowed into the Peiraeus, the port of Athens. The combination of her trade supremacy and the tribute from her empire made Athens one of the richest of the Greek cities of her day.

It was a very modest wealth from the modern point of view.

The total annual state revenue of Periclean Athens in peace-time was probably close to 1,000 talents. . . . In terms of its purchasing power today . . . that is about the annual budget of a fair-sized Canadian city.

During the Peloponnesian War the tribute from the empire was raised and resort was had to the *eisphora,* or direct property tax. Even in peace-time, though there were no schools, hospitals, or old-age pensions to drain the public purse, the treasury had to take care of the public festivals such as the Panathenaea and the two Dionysia—which were drama festivals—and of the huge program of non-productive public works, such as the Parthenon. In addition, from 17,000 to 20,000 of the 43,000 citizens 'ate state bread'—that is, they were on public service and were paid for it.

Their pay was not large. Jurymen, for example, got two and later three *obols* a day. . . . *Hoplites* [infantry soldiers] received four *obols* . . . a day, sailors and marines only three *obols.*

And so one might go on. Athens could scarcely have balanced her budget, had it not been for the liturgies. These were of various kinds, of which two are of particular interest. In the *choregia* a rich man was picked to collect, maintain, instruct, and equip one of the many choruses needed, for (among other forms of art) the drama. This might cost him as much as half a talent. . . . The *trierarchia* was more expensive. In it a rich man had to pay the cost of operating a *trireme* for a year. The cost was between two-thirds of a talent to a talent.

All citizens who owned property worth more than three talents . . . were subject to the liturgies. In the first years of the Peloponnesian War, the generals were able to find 400 *trierarchs* a year.

The liturgies were a capital tax on the rich, both citizens and *metics.* Yet we learn that in Periclean Athens the holders of them competed against each other to provide the best-trained chorus or the most splendidly equipped *trireme.*

The Athenians were not in love with poverty. Pericles himself in his *Funeral Speech* observed: 'We think it no disgrace to confess to poverty but a disgrace to make no effort to overcome it.'

But the whole training of an Athenian encouraged him to put simple recreations and an active life of the imagination above possessions; and he also took it for granted that citizenship involved duties as well as rights.

The Original Olympic Games

Judith Swaddling

Olympia, located in southwestern Greece, was the site of the most prestigious and popular athletic competition held in ancient times. Judith Swaddling, of the Department of Greek and Roman Antiquities at the British Museum, compiled the following important background information on the ancient Olympic festival and games. She describes the physical setting of the site and also the structures that made up the sacred Olympic sanctuary (the Altis, dedicated to Zeus). She also tells about how the games started (including the legends the Greeks passed on about their founding), the Olympic truce, the organizers (from the city-state of Elis), how the athletes trained, and the grand procession from Elis to the Altis. Swaddling then provides a general program of the activities and athletic events of the festival's five days, approximately the way scholars think they occurred in the late Classical Age. The footraces included the *stade* (about 600 feet); the *diaulos* (two *stades* in length); the *dolichos* (about twenty-four *stades* in length); and the *hoplitodromos* (a race in armor, about two *stades* in length). There was a horse race for jockeys who rode bareback and two chariot races—the *tethrippon* (for four-horse chariots) and *synoris* (for two-horse chariots). The three combat events were wrestling, boxing, and the *pankration* (a rough-and-tumble combination of wrestling and boxing). In addition, the pentathlon consisted of five events: discus throw, javelin throw, broad jump, wrestling, and the *stade;* and there were boys' versions of many of these same events. (It should be noted that some other events were introduced but later discontinued; for instance, the *apene,* a race for mule-carts, first appeared on the program in 500 B.C., but was dropped in 444 B.C.)

Every fourth year for a thousand years, from 776 BC to AD 395, the pageantry of the Olympic festival attracted citizens

Judith Swaddling, *The Ancient Olympic Games*. Austin: University of Texas Press, 1980. Copyright © 1980 by The Trustees of the British Museum. Reproduced by permission.

from all over the Greek world. They flocked to Olympia, the permanent setting for the Games, in the early years coming in their hundreds from neighbouring towns and city-states, and later in their thousands by land and sea from colonies as far away as Spain and Africa. . . . What drew them all this way to endure the discomforts which Epictetus records? The Games, of course, and perhaps no less the celebratory banquets that followed, but there was something more . . .

The Sacred Altis

The Games were held in honour of the god Zeus, the supreme god of Greek mythology, and a visit to Olympia was also a pilgrimage to his most sacred place, the grove known as the Altis. There is no modern parallel for Olympia; it would have to be a site combining a sports complex and a centre for religious devotion, something like a combination of Wembley Stadium and Westminster Abbey.

Olympia is situated in a fertile, grassy plain on the north bank of the broad river Alpheios, just to the east of its confluence with the Kladeos, which rushes down to meet it from the mountains of Elis. In ancient times the area was pleasantly shaded with plane and olive-trees, white poplars and even palm-trees, while vines and flowering shrubs grew thickly beneath them. Rising above the site, to the north, is the lofty, pine-covered hill of Kronos, named after the father of Zeus. Successive waves of peoples who passed through the area in prehistoric times each observed the sanctity of this hallowed area. Modern visitors to the site often express surprise that the Games were held in such a remote area, but in antiquity, the river Alpheios was navigable, and Olympia was easily accessible both from the sea (it was about fifteen kilometres from the coast) and by means of inland routes converging on the site. The hill of Kronos must always have been a conspicuous landmark in the surrounding terrain.

The clearing within the grove at the foot of the hill was once associated with fertility rites. . . . Gradually, as the worship of Zeus became predominant, people began to honour him at simple altars in the grove and hung their offerings—primitive terracotta and bronze figurines of men and animals—on the branches of nearby trees. With the establishment of the Games, this sanctuary grew and flourished. From the sixth century BC onwards the Altis was gradually adorned with temples, treasuries, halls, elaborate altars and literally hundreds of marble and bronze statues. The statues, some of which were several times life-size, were mostly victory dedications to Zeus for athletic and military achievements, and were set up by both states and individuals. There were also monuments erected in honour of benefactors, and offerings of costly materials given by wealthy tyrants and princes. Most remarkable of all the spectacles at Olympia was one of the 'Seven Wonders of the World': the resplendent thirteen-metre-high gold and ivory statue of Zeus within his magnificent temple. The statue was the work of Pheidias, the great sculptor of the fifth century BC.

As regards the origin of the Olympic Games, one can, as often in Greek history, either believe the legends, of which there are many, or look for a more down-to-earth beginning. According to the poet Pindar, Olympia was virtually created by Herakles, the 'superman' of Greek mythology. He made a clearing in the grove, laid out the boundaries of the Altis and instituted the first games in honour of Zeus. His purpose was to celebrate the success of one of his twelve labours, the cleaning of the cattle stables of King Augeas of Elis, which had been achieved by diverting the river Alpheios from its course. It is more likely, however, that athletic festivals like the Olympic Games developed from the funeral games which were held in honour of local heroes. Pelops . . . was the local hero of Olympia, and his grave and sanctuary were situated within the Altis. It is interesting that he was said to come from the east, for many people believe that it was in Asia Minor that the first organised athletic contests took place, when the Greek communities established there became prosperous enough to devote their leisure time to sport. At that time mainland Greece was still unsettled by wars and migrations.

The Olympic Truce

The traditional date for the establishment of the Olympic Games was 776 BC, but competitions appear to have been held on an unofficial basis long before this. King Iphitos of Elis, a shadowy figure who lived around the ninth century BC, is said to have re-instituted the Games on the advice of the Delphic Oracle. The king had asked the Oracle how to bring an end to the civil wars and pestilence which were gradually destroying the land of Greece, whereupon the priestess advised that he should restore the Olympic Games and declare a truce for their duration. Whether this is true or not the Olympic Truce was a major instrument in the unification of the Greek states and colonies.

In order to spread the news of the Truce before the beginning of the Olympic festival, three heralds decked with olive wreaths and carrying staffs were sent out from Elis to every Greek state. It was the heralds' duty to announce the exact date of the festival, to invite the inhabitants to attend and, most important of all, to announce the Olympic Truce. In this way they came to be known as the Truce-Bearers, *Spondophoroi*; they served not only as heralds but also as full-time legal advisers to the Eleans. Originally the Truce lasted for one month but it was extended to two and then three months, to protect visitors coming from further afield. The terms of the Truce were engraved on a bronze discus which was kept in the Temple of Hera in the Altis. It forbade states participating in the Games to take up arms, to pursue legal disputes or to carry out death penalties. This was to ensure that pilgrims and athletes travelling to and from Olympia would have a safe journey. Violators of the Truce were heavily fined, and indeed on one occasion, Alexander the Great himself had to recompense an Athenian who was robbed by some of his mercenaries whilst travelling to Olympia.

The Olympic Games are the oldest of the four panhellenic or national athletic festivals which composed the *periodos* or 'circuit' games. The other three were the Pythian Games at Delphi, held in honour of Apollo, the Isthmian Games held at Corinth for Poseidon, and the Games at Nemea, which, like the Olympics, were in honour of Zeus. A major distraction between the Greek games and our own is that all major and minor athletic festivals, of which several hundred had been established by Roman times, were celebrated under the patronage of a divinity. The god was believed to bestow on the athletes the physical prowess which enabled them to take part in the Games. Accordingly, the athletes prayed to the deity and promised offerings should they be victorious.

The Olympic festival was celebrated once every four years in accordance with the Greek calendar, which was based on the lunar month. It was always timed so that the central day of the festival coincided with the second or third full moon after the summer solstice. This may well indicate the assimilation at some stage of the Games with fertility rites which celebrated the harvesting. It is often asked why the Greeks should have chosen the very hottest time of the year, mid-August or mid-September, for such strenuous exertion. Apart from the lunar associations it surely made sense to hold the Games at the one time during the year when work on the land was at a standstill. By then the crops were gathered and there was a lull in which men were eager to relax and celebrate the end of a hard year's work. . . .

The Stadium

The stadium did not exist during the early years of the Olympic Games. The athletes made use of an open level stretch of ground with a line drawn in the sand to mark the start (giving rise to our term 'starting from scratch'). As the races were held in honour of the god Zeus, it was appropriate that the finishing line should be close to his altar. The spectators stood on the lower slopes of the hill of Kronos.

These simple arrangements were adequate for the first centuries of the Olympic Games. Gradually various improvements were made and a rudimentary stadium was constructed within the Altis. It had shallow banks and a rectangular track, for, unlike ours, all ancient races were run on the straight. Eventually, around 350 BC a magnificent new stadium was constructed and it was situated, significantly, outside the Altis boundaries. By this time the games, although still part of the religious festival, had become established in their own right. Originally Zeus had been glorified for granting powers of strength and physical endurance to the athletes; now the athletes were becoming increasingly professional and beginning to gain recognition as cult figures themselves. Thus the removal of the stadium from the sacred precinct was a development in religious as well as athletic history.

The track in the stadium was of clay, levelled and lightly covered with sand. It had stone sills towards each end which marked the start and finish of the races. To preserve some of the religious significance of the games it was desirable for all races to finish at the western end of the course, so that the runners still ran towards the heart of the Altis as they had done in the early days. Races consisting of an even number of lengths were therefore started at the western end. The course was separated from the embankment by a ridge of stone blocks, to the outside of which was a channel that conducted water round the stadium, discharging at intervals into basins for the refreshment of spectators who stood all day in the blazing sun without any shelter.

The length of the track at Olympia is six hundred Olympic feet, 192.28 metres. According to mythology, Herakles fixed the distance of the original race (and ultimately of the stadium) by placing one foot in front of the other six hundred times. An alternative explanation was that Herakles was able to run this distance in one breath before pausing to take another. Thus it has been suggested that 'stadium' was derived from the Greek word 'to stand.' All ancient stadia were approximately six hundred feet in length but most places used a local standard of measure, causing a slight variation in the length of each stadium.

The ground rose naturally in the east and artificial embankments were constructed in the north, west and south, requiring an immense amount of labour. In this way a surprising total of between forty and forty-five thousand spectators could be accommodated. To afford spectators an uninterrupted view of the race the two long embankments were designed so that they were three metres further apart at the centre than at the ends. This arrangement is found in other ancient stadia and was copied in the modern Olympic stadium in Athens. . . .

Preparation and Training

The Olympic Festival lasted for five days but the preparations took virtually the whole of the preceding year. Strangely, there is no firm evidence that the sports facilities at Olympia were used during the period between the festivals. Local villagers may have exercised there but they would have been few in number. Much hard physical labour was therefore required to get things ready. Any undergrowth that had sprung up had to be cleared. The courses had to be dug and levelled and the sand pits prepared. Repairs and general tidying up of the buildings and monuments in and around the sanctuary were also necessary.

The most important officials at the Games, who were known

as the *Hellanodikai*, commenced preparations ten months before the games were due to start. Their name means literally 'judges

---

A Poet Glorifies a Winning Athlete

This is an excerpt from the Sixth Nemean Ode, *by Pindar (born ca. 518 B.C.), an important Greek poet who wrote a large number of* epinikia, *odes honoring victorious athletes. The piece celebrates Alkimidas of Aegina, a young man who won the boys' wrestling about 461 B.C. The poem begins with a sweeping statement about the gods and how a few humans, notably gifted athletes, might emulate them. Then Pindar singles out Alkimidas by setting his victory amid those of prior games winners, including some of his own ancestors.*

Single is the race, single
Of men and of gods;
From a single mother we both draw breath.
But a difference of power in everything
Keeps us apart;
For the one [humanity] is as Nothing, but the brazen sky [abode
    of the gods]
Stays a fixed habitation for ever.
Yet we can in greatness of mind
Or of body be like the Immortals,
Tho' we know not to what goal
By day or in the nights
Fate has written that we shall run.

Even now Alkimidas gives visible witness
That his race is like the fruitful fields
Which change about
And now give men abounding life from the soil,
Now rest again and pick up strength.
He has come from Nemea's well-loved Games,
A boy in the struggle,
Who follows this calling from Zeus;
He has been revealed a hunter
And had good sport in the wrestling.

He plants his feet in the kindred tracks
Of his father's father, Praxidamas;
For he, an Olympian victor,
First brought twigs from Alpheos to the Aiakidai.

Pindar, *Sixth Nemean Ode*, in *Pindar: Odes*, trans. C.M. Bowra. New York: Penguin, 1969, pp. 206–209.

of the Greeks', reflecting the national character of the Games. In the early years of the festival they had been referred to merely as *agonothetai*, 'games organisers'. They had their own special residence in Elis called the *hellanodikaion*. The Hellanodikai were chosen by lot, and although their numbers fluctuated, there were ten for most of the history of the Games. One of them acted as the overall supervisor while the rest were divided into three groups, each presiding over different events. The first group organised the equestrian events, the second the pentathlon, and the third the remainder of the competitions. Throughout the ages the Olympic judges were renowned for their impartiality. They wore robes of purple, the royal colour serving as a reminder of the time when King Iphitos controlled the Games and officiated as the sole judge. The athletes, too, had to be in strict training in their home towns during the ten months prior to the Games and they had to swear to this effect.

For at least one month before the festival prospective competitors in the Games were required to reside at Elis and train under the strict supervision of the Hellanodikai. There were three gymnasiums at Elis and in addition the local market place was stripped and used as a practice track for the horse races. This period of compulsory training at Elis was enforced by the Eleans probably to demonstrate their absolute control over the Games. Their authority had been contested in the past particularly by their neighbours the Pisatans, but eventually the Eleans established supremacy. During this month the judges were fully occupied with various tasks: they disqualified those who were not fit, checked on parentage and Greek descent, and resolved any disputes concerning the classification of men and boys, horses and colts. The training was renowned for its harshness: the athletes had to observe a strict diet, carry out a gruelling regime of exercise and obey every word of the Hellanodikai. It is not certain when the period of compulsory training was introduced, but since it required the athlete to be away from home for a considerable time he had to be fairly affluent. Sometimes his father or brother would accompany him to Elis but more often a private trainer had to be employed. By this time the era of the amateur athlete was clearly coming to a close.

Two days before the festival began the whole company set out from Elis, which was roughly fifty-eight kilometres from Olympia. First came the Hellanodikai and other officials, then the athletes and their trainers, horses and chariots together with their owners, jockeys and charioteers. They followed the Sacred Way along the coast, stopping to sacrifice a pig and to perform other rites at the fountain of Piera on the boundary between Elis and Olympia. They spent the night at Letrini and the next day wound their way along the valley of the Alpheios towards the Altis.

Meanwhile people from all walks of life had been making their way to Olympia. Princes and tyrants from Sicily and southern Italy sailed up the river in splendid barges; ambassadors came from various towns, vying with each other in dress and paraphernalia. The rich came on horseback, and in chariots; the poor came on donkeys, in carts and even on foot. Food-sellers came loaded with supplies for there was no town near Olympia. Merchants flocked in with their wares. Artisans came to make figurines that pilgrims could buy to offer to their god. Booths and stalls were set up; tents and huts were erected, for only official delegates were given accommodation in the magnificent guesthouse known as the *Leonidaion*. Most visitors looked for a suitable spot to put down their belongings and slept each night under the summer skies. . . .

The Olympic Programme

Day One   **Morning** Swearing-in ceremony for competitors and judges in the Boulcuterion (Council-House) before the altar and statue of Zeus *Horkios* (Zeus of the Oaths).
Contests for heralds and trumpeters held near the stadium entrance.
Boys' running, wrestling and boxing contests.
Public and private prayers and sacrifices in the Altis;
consultation of oracles.
Afternoon Orations by well-known philosophers and recitals by poets and historians.
Sightseeing tours of the Altis.
Reunions with old friends.

Day Two   **Morning** Procession into the hippodrome of all those competing there.

Chariot- and horse-races.

Afternoon The pentathlon: discus, javelin, jumping, running and wrestling.

Evening Funeral rites in honour of the hero Pelops.

Parade of victors round the Altis.

Communal singing of victory hymns.

Feasting and revelry.

Day Three   **Morning** Procession of the Hellanodikai (Judges), ambassadors from the Greek states, competitors in all events and sacrificial animals round the Altis to the Great Altar in front of the Temple of Zeus, followed by the official sacrifice of one hundred oxen given by the people of Elis.

Afternoon Foot-races.

Evening Public banquet in the Prytaneion.

Day Four   **Morning** Wrestling.

Midday Boxing and the *pankration.*

Afternoon Race-in-armour.

Day Five   Procession of victors to the Temple of Zeus where they are crowned with wreaths of wild olive by the Hellanodikai, followed by the *phyllobolia* (when the victors are showered with leaves and flowers).

Feasting and celebrations.

Arts and Medicine

CHAPTER

3

Chapter Preface

Today when people talk about or prepare to visit Greece, no other aspect of its ancient culture inspires more interest, anticipation, and pure joy as its surviving examples of classic art and architecture. Chief among these is the magnificent temple complex atop Athens's central hill, the Acropolis. Even in its present advanced state of ruin, the centerpiece of the complex—the Parthenon, temple of Athena, the city's patron deity—regularly elicits feelings of amazement and awe in all who visit it in person. Phidias, the greatest sculptor of the ancient world, designed its splendid sculptures; and thousands of Athenians of all walks of life labored for years to erect this soaring monument to the human spirit.

Athens was not the only city-state to raise such temples, however. The remains of hundreds of others dot the Greek countryside, along with expertly rendered statues ranging from tiny figurines to larger-than-life-size masterpieces. Potters also helped to define the creative output of Greek art over the centuries. Ceramics became a major industry in many city-states, turning out hundreds of thousands of vases, cups, bowls, and other vessels for both public and private use; but these objects were, more often than not, works of art as well as utilitarian products. Scenes painted on vases and other pottery artifacts captured numerous aspects of daily life, worship, and war with a wonderful combination of precision, simplicity, and beauty.

Another aspect of ancient Greece's creative output was its unique and highly influential exploration of ideas, an endeavor that stimulated the birth of Western philosophy, science, literature, and medicine. In addition to the many scholarly treatises turned out by thinkers and writers ranging from the scientists Thales, Pythagoras, Democritus, and Archimedes, to the historians Herodotus and Thucydides, to the philosophers Socrates, Plato, Aristotle, and Epicurus, local medical schools arose. The most famous and influential of these schools was the one founded by Hippocrates, now viewed as the father of Western medicine. He and his followers made the seminal observation that health and disease have natural rather than supernatural explanations. Like Greek art, architecture, and philosophy, Greek medicine helped to form the foundations of modern Western thinking.

Constructing the Parthenon

Peter Green

Raising the Parthenon, arguably the most magnificent temple of ancient times, was a tremendous cooperative effort that involved Athenians and other Greeks of all walks of life and levels of work skills. Leading the small army of builders was Pericles, an Athenian general and politician and the most influential Greek leader of mid-fifth-century B.C. Greece. Constructing a mighty complex of temples and shrines on the Acropolis, both to honor the goddess Athena and shout Athenian imperial greatness to the world, was his idea and he expended relentless enthusiasm and energy to ensure the project was funded and on track. Below him were the master artists who designed the building and its sculptures, including the architect Iktinos, and especially Phidias, now viewed as the finest sculptor of the ancient world. Then came numerous artisans and craftspeople, from stonemasons and woodcarvers to metalsmiths and painters, some of whom were Athenian and others who came from other city-states. Finally, hundreds and sometimes thousands of ordinary Athenians lent their hands and backs to the considerable unskilled labor force needed to erect a structure of such size. Noted classical historian Peter Green here surveys the methods used to raise the Parthenon, as well as its major features. He also provides insights into some of the builders, notably Phidias, whose sad fate following the temple's completion shows that in every great endeavor, however noble, someone always ends up paying a price.

It took two years of detailed planning before all specifications were approved, every contract for labor and materials let, and work on the Parthenon could actually begin. The first stone was laid on July 28, 447, during the Panathenaic festival. Separate boards of overseers were appointed for the temple and its cult

Peter Green, *The Parthenon*. New York: Newsweek Book Division, 1973. Copyright © 1973 by Arnoldo Mondadori Editore, S.p.A. Reproduced by permission of Newsweek, Inc.

statue, the importance—and cost—of which should not be un-derestimated. To the casual observer it must have seemed that Pericles envisaged no more than an elaborate restoration of the Older Parthenon, on the same foundation base and with roughly identical dimensions. Such observations woefully underestimated Phidias and his associates, however, for although they reused blocks wherever possible they also built throughout in the pure white Pentelic marble, an unprecedented extravagance.

Exterior and Interior Design

The same expansive attitude can be seen in their treatment of the Parthenon's overall proportions. The normal Doric temple had six columns in its façade and thirteen down each side. This ratio—of $6 : 6 \times 2 + 1$—was disrupted in certain cases, the two Parthenons included, by the ritual need for an extra chamber be-yond the cella [main room holding the god's cult statue], which made for a long, narrow floor plan. Here the architects of the Parthenon completely broke with tradition. Rather than merely increase the number of columns in the peristyle [enclosure of columns], they broadened the façade to eight columns—thus restoring the proportional ratio—and similarly extended the cella. To avoid any impression of squat lumpishness, the columns of the façade were made finer and taller than the Doric norm and set uncharacteristically close together.

Among other things, this innovation enabled Phidias to ex-periment with interior space when executing and siting his colos-sal cult statue of Athena. Rather than place it tamely and con-ventionally against the back wall of the cella, he set its base well forward, isolating it further by means of an internal peristyle. The construction of this image, reputedly almost forty feet in height, base included, must in itself have been a formidable undertak-ing. A huge vertical beam, rising from a central floor socket, served as an armature [inner support frame]. To support the statue's arms, Phidias may have employed an iron core inserted through the vertical beam at the point of balance. The statue it-self was then built up by means of shaped and bonded wooden blocks held to the armature by internal struts. Over this surface, finally, was fitted a sheath of gold and ivory plates. The gold plates, reasonably enough, were made detachable for inspection, since they came from state funds and were worth a king's ransom. Ivory was used on the feet, hands, and face to represent the goddess's flesh—an appropriate choice, for it was both milk pale and costly. Athena's eyes glinted with gems; her left hand rested on her shield, and in her right she held aloft a crowned [statue of the goddess] Victory. Above her helmet, between winged griffins, crouched an inscrutable sphinx. The overall effect . . . must have been nothing short of overwhelming—if a trifle garish for modern taste.

Quarrying and Transporting the Stones

The first year of construction was consumed almost entirely with quarrying and transporting marble from Mount Pentelicus—that pure white, finely grained stone that, because of its slight iron content, weathers to the pale honey gold so characteristic of the Parthenon itself. This part of the work, too often ignored or taken for granted, presented formidable obstacles that were overcome only with extraordinary ingenuity. One can still see the chisel marks where rectangular blocks were first cut and then split away from the rest of the excavation by means of water-soaked—and consequently expanding—wooden wedges. More hazardous still

The roof and interior walls of the Parthenon are missing now, but the mighty outer colonnade and some sculptures remain.

was the business of transportation, especially during the first stages, when the quarried blocks had to be brought down a steep and rocky mountainside from heights of between two and three thousand feet. The blocks had to be maneuvered on sleds down a paved quarry road (parts of which still survive), and only the smaller ones could be eased along on rollers. At intervals there were stout posts, carrying rope and tackle, which were used to help brake the sleds' downward momentum. Accidents were not unknown, and one rough-dressed column drum, probably destined for the Parthenon, lies in a nearby ravine to this day.

Even when the plain was safely reached, difficulties still abounded. Shifting a total of 22,000 tons of marble across ten miles of level plain to the Acropolis proved a major operation in itself. These drums, blocks, and architraves were so enormously heavy that special methods of transport had to be devised for them, and the existing road had to be rebuilt so that it was strong enough to support their weight. Traffic was restricted to the dry summer months for fear that the blocks would bog down in the mud, and the largest blocks of all seem to have baffled the wagonmakers. Axles had to be inserted directly into their end sockets, and these were then equipped with wheels no less than twelve feet in diameter. The whole was fitted to a frame of four-inch timbers and drawn by up to thirty teams of oxen. Shifting a block of marble from the quarry to the Acropolis took at least two days and cost up to 300 drachmas—at a time when one drachma was the average laborer's daily wage. Then, at the foot of the Acropolis itself there was more sweating with sleds and rollers, pulleys and tackle before the blocks could finally be maneuvered into position atop the citadel for the stonemasons to dress.

All Sorts of Workers

"So the buildings arose," says [the first-century A.D. Greek biographer] Plutarch, "as imposing in their sheer size as they were inimitable in the grace of their outlines, since the artists strove to excel themselves in the beauty of their workmanship." Highly skilled sculptors and masons worked diligently year after year for what were surely, even by contemporary standards, little more than day-laborers' wages. There is a story . . . that when one of the overtired wagon mules was turned loose for a rest, it came back to the works of its own accord, trotting alongside its yoke-mates and even leading the way for them, as though exhorting and inciting them on. The Assembly purportedly decreed that so enthusiastically patriotic a beast should be maintained at public expense for the rest of its life, like a victorious athlete.

Not all such displays of goodwill were as altruistic, however. As Pericles had foreseen, the project provided employment for all sorts of workers over a number of years, and there can have been few citizens who failed to draw some benefit from it, if only indirectly. Athenians became inured to the endless clink of hammer and chisel, to overseers shouting orders, and to the sight of long dusty teams of oxen plodding up the Panathenaic Way with their massive loads of freshly cut marble bright against the cobalt sky.

A Sense of Dynamic Tension

At first, work on the Parthenon seems to have moved slowly. Indeed, the first three years were largely spent quarrying blocks and drums [round components of the columns] and laying out the courses of the stylobate [the temple's foundation]. This last was a particularly tricky operation because Phidias and his associates planned a very slight convex curvature in the horizontal line of the temple's base, one that would affect all other horizontals throughout the structure. As a result, the shape of the stylobate had to be precisely right; a whole system of subtle optical illusion depended on it.

Paradoxically, nothing in formal architecture looks less straight than a straight line; vertically it wilts, horizontally it sags. In a temple the size of the Parthenon this created a very real problem. Armed with mathematical expertise and remarkable aesthetic flair, Phidias and his two fellow architects set out to defeat the shortcomings of the human eye. Not only the stylobate, but also the columns rising from it were given a gentle, swelling curve. More striking still, these columns were all made to lean fractionally inward toward the cella, thus creating an impression of soaring perspective. (It has been calculated that if extended upward those columns would converge at a point one and a half miles above the Acropolis.) Variations in the spacing of columns and metopes added depth and solidity to the façades, and other refinements enhanced the overall visual impression, creating a sense of dynamic tension. . . .

A Riot of Color and Decoration

Work on the Parthenon's metopes [rectangular sculpted panels on the sides of the structure] and frieze [continuous sculpted panel running around the perimeter beneath the roof] continued throughout this building period. The great cult statue of Athena was likewise progressing, and only the sculptures on the pediments [triangular gables beneath the roof on the building's ends] had to wait until the rest of the temple was complete. In 440 the great doors were set in place—and subsequently embellished with the most elaborate ornamentation. Paneled and studded in bronze with animal heads, ivory inlay, and gold rosettes adorning the panels themselves, these doors formed a worthy entrance to the shrine. Roof beams, coffered ceilings, and wooden grilles were also now set in place; the giant statue, complete at last, gleamed on its plinth; and at the Panathenaic festival of 438, less than ten years after their inception, temple and statue were formally dedicated to Athena.

We are so accustomed to the chaste and broken whiteness of those timeworn columns that it is hard for us to envisage the Parthenon as it looked upon its completion. Time has removed all trace of color from its stones, but perhaps that is just as well for modern taste, since the Greeks had a passion for gilding or painting any stone surface in sight, and the Parthenon received more gilt than most. Its sculptures were especially lavishly decorated, with colored glass added to highlight eyes, for example. The apex of each pediment sprouted huge, writhing stone tendrils and acanthus leaves, and moldings ran riot. The general impression was, first and foremost, of an almost baroque clutter, hubris [pride] sanctified by religion and justified through art. . . .

A Sculptor's Fate

Understandably, no single item in the entire building program aroused as much hostile criticism as Phidias's statue. If the concept bespoke megalomania, the cost suggested pure spendthrift lunacy. Over 2,500 pounds of gold—worth more than 3,500,000 drachmas—had gone into it, and another 1,386,000 drachmas had been expended on ivory, wood, sculptors' fees, and miscellaneous expenses. By any estimate the total bill far outstripped the cost of the Parthenon itself. Small wonder then that despite the most stringent official precautions wild rumors of large-scale graft and embezzlement circulated during the statue's construction. Immediately after the dedication, charges were brought against Phidias, and vigorous efforts were made to involve Pericles himself in the scandal. Libelous fragments preserved from comedies of the day show that the political opposition, though crippled, had by no means given up. Phidias reportedly detached and weighed the gold plates to prove his innocence, but feelings were running so high that he judged it advisable to leave town in some haste rather than stand trial. He went to Olympia, where a commission for a giant statue of Zeus awaited him. His last workshop, complete with signed drinking mug and the molds he used to fashion metal drapery, has recently been discovered in Olympia, where, probably in 433, the sculptor died without ever having returned to Athens.

Pottery Craftsmanship

Thomas Craven

Ceramics, or pottery-making, was long one of Greece's chief industries. Using hands-on techniques inherited from artisans of prior centuries, the master potters of the Classical Age molded wet clay (*ceramos*) on wheels and fired it in kilns reaching a temperature of 1000 degrees Fahrenheit. Usually, they crafted their wares for practical use; yet they also strove for originality of design and excellence of execution in every piece. The late, noted art historian, Thomas Craven, here examines the major Greek pottery styles employed before and during the Classical Age, including geometric, black-figure, and red-figure. He also names and describes the major kinds of vessels the potters produced.

The master potters of the world were the Greeks. In variety, design, productivity, and the adaptation of beautifully made objects to everyday use, they have left . . . us . . . many thousands of examples of their highest skill. . . .

The tradition of Greek pottery had its historical origin in the palaces of Crete . . . as early as 2500 B.C. During this luxury-loving age, a school of superb geometrical vase-making was followed by free, or anti-symmetrical, pottery, the motifs of which were largely biological-plants, jellyfish, octopi, and other small fauna. In the ninth and eighth centuries B.C., there was a return to geometrical design, in some respects memorable, but for the most part monotonous and unimaginative. The basements of museums have innumerable exhibits of this period in the glass cases behind the mummies and the plaster casts. The resurgent geometrical style was applied to large urns and vases of every shape and capacity. Generally speaking, it was a scheme of ornamentation in which single, or concentric circles predominated, the circles broken, crossed by tangential lines, and interlacings, to divert the eye from round-and-round tracings. Between the circular bands, on the larger vases, were crude pictures of naval engagements and

Thomas Craven, *The Pocket Books of Greek Art*. New York: Pocket Books, 1950. Copyright © 1950 by Thomas Craven. Reproduced by permission of Simon and Schuster, Inc.

funeral processions—events noticed ceremonially at the double gate of Athens, the Dipylon gate, which gave its name to the style. The color scheme of the ninth and eighth century vases consisted of reddish-brown figures, accentuated by white or black touches, against a ground of pale yellow or buff tones.

The Black-Figure Style

For a full century, from 600 to 500 B.C., the potters labored in the black-figure style—that is, with dark linear figures set against an earthen-red ground. The figures were drawn in the archaic tradition; but decoratively as pattern-components placed on the belly of an urn, they put modern ceramists to shame. The black-figure style is . . . indeed, in design and proportioning, a beautiful form of ceramics. The word ceramics, incidentally, comes from the name of a locality near Athens where potters' clay was obtained—but it is hardly in the same class as the red-figure ware. Before looking at the classic style, it will be useful to review the geometrical shapes first employed by the Greeks.

For storing or carrying wine and other liquids, the *amphora*, a vase with a narrow neck and handles on each side below the neck, was in common use. The water jar was the *hydria*, a vessel equipped with three handles and broader at the shoulder than the *amphora*. The *crater*, broad-rimmed with short cylindrical supports, was the mixing bowl and a favorite vase in Renaissance Florence. Varieties of the *crater*, such as the cup and the bell, were popular and in constant demand.

Black-figure vase-painting was followed, about 500 B.C., by a different method which simply reversed the traditional procedure. The reversed technique was the far-flung red-figure style, in which the ground was covered with lustrous black pigment and the figures composed in red, in the natural terra-cotta tones of the clay, or brightened by some warm earth tones. The red-figure style was enormously fecund [fertile], and vase-painters enjoyed a fame second only to that of sculptors. Boldly they signed their works, and today you may see inscriptions in capital letters on many of the objects. I wondered about those inscriptions until I was proficient enough to translate them, and more often than not, they were shameless bouquets from the master potter to an apprentice chosen because of his physical comeliness. They read as a rule something like this: *Young Skouras Is a Handsome Lad;* or *That Boy Aristophanes Is the Playmate of Zeus;* or *Erysipelas is the Apple of My Eye.*

Practical, Yet Beautiful

The Greeks made pottery for utilitarian purposes, but as in all their works of art, they would tolerate nothing this side of per-

Greek pottery was designed to be both useful and decorative, and most individual pieces were unique.

fection; and even in the mass production period at Athens, after the Peloponnesian War, and in the colonies, they never duplicated a design or stole a motif. The problems occupying them in their pottery and their domestic implements were identical, though on a more modest scale, with those of temple-building and carving—infinite simplicity, free but perfect proportioning, functionalism, or the adaptation of shape and form to intended purpose—and above all others, a beautiful sense of fitness which was never corrupted by melodramatic tricks or sensationalism.

The wares of the Greek ceramists were part and parcel of the routine life of the people. Vases were designed to hold flowers and fruits, or as decanters for wine, or as storage jars. Beautiful cups were fashioned for drinking purposes and all sorts of table china were decorated with religious scenes. The ceremonials in the temples and at *al fresco* [outdoor] altars necessitated a great variety of sacred vessels; the holy olive oil given as a prize in the Panathenaic games required a container of impeccable artistry, as did those of other festivities such as a special form of *amphora*, with a long neck, which held the water for the bridal bath—and was also used as a monument for those who died unmarried. The exquisitely shaped *lecythus*, a bell-mouthed, narrow-necked, single-handed vase, was filled with fragrant oils and buried with the dead or left at the grave side.

To a large extent, the vases and pottery in use today are derived from Greek models, whether they come from the celebrated designers of Sweden and France, or from the factories owned by the dime stores. With the classic Athenians, ceramic art in its decorative aspects was purely decorative in most cases, but with the masters, it was also a medium for the delineation, on a small scale, of the mural paintings of the great decorators. In fact, the murals of the *Stoa* [a long, columned building in the Athenian marketplace], by Polygnotus, are known solely from the small-scale adaptations on vases and urns.

The Greeks, as a matter of course, ornamented their vases and household implements with subject matter of a religious nature—or with scenes from decisive battles in which the issue turned on the will of the gods. . . .

I do not wish to imply that all the religious motifs employed by the old potters were executed in a spirit of reverence. The re-

Polygnotus: Master Artist

The master potters decorated their wares with stunning linear paintings depicting scenes from mythology, wars, and everyday life. Often these paintings copied or were influenced by portions of large wall murals painted by master artists such as Polygnotus (flourished ca. 475–447 B.C.), who hailed from the northern Aegean island of Thasos. One of his stylistic innovations was to spread his figures across the painting, rather than in a single line, the most common method of earlier painters. To indicate depth, he placed some of his figures above the others, giving the impression they were farther away. Ancient writers praised him for the boldness of his scenes, which frequently featured humans in the midst of action, their faces alive with emotion.

Polygnotus's most famous painting, which unfortunately has not survived, was the Capture of Troy, *displayed at Delphi (home of the famous oracle of the god Apollo). Though the work itself has long since vanished, fortunately its general look has survived; the later ancient Greek traveler Pausanias described it in his guidebook, saying in part:*

As you go into the building [the so-called "club-house," which long housed some of Polygnotus's finest works] on the right is the painting that shows the fall of Troy and the Greeks sailing away. Menelaus's men are getting ready for the voyage [back to Greece]; there is a painting of the ship with a mixture of men and boys among the sailors, and the ship's steersman Phrontis standing amidships holding two poles. . . . [Some men] are taking down Menelaus's tent not far from the ship. . . . Briseis is standing with Diomedes above her and Iphis in front of them as if they are all gazing at Helen's beauty. Helen herself is standing with Eurybates near her. . . . Above Helen sits a man wrapped in a purple cloak, extremely melancholy; you would know it was Priam's son Helenos even before you read the inscription.

Pausanias's quote taken from Pausanias, *Guide to Greece,* trans. Peter Levi. 2 vols. New York: Penguin, 1971, vol. 1, pp. 469–71.

ligion of the Greeks was open to all manner of excitements from profound worship to pure sensuality, and on many of the choicest examples of vase-making, you may see fiercely amorous satyrs approaching reclining maidens in attitudes which would never pass a modern censor. The most prevalent subjects are variations on the power and personal habits of the gods, or on the Homeric and Persian wars. In hundreds and hundreds of vases you will see the Amazons holding their own against undersize *hoplites*; Heracles dining with Athena, or diverting himself with female warriors, the gods feasting, relaxing, or plotting trouble on earth, revelers headed by Dionysus, satyrs pursuing maenads, and young athletes in training or in competition. . . .

Linear Artists

The Greeks, proceeding from black figures to red, and from archaic postures and draftsmanship, to the free and cultivated and precise style of the fourth century B.C., created the most beautiful linear designs ever drawn upon pottery. Their drawings at the peak of the classic period, both on a black ground, and in rarer examples now more valuable than any other ceramics, on a white ground, have been admired and adapted by western artists. . . .

In the mature, classic vase-painting, the old artists did not attempt to produce realistic effects, or the modern technical devices of three-dimensional figures, seen in perspective. They were linear artists [those working mainly in one dimension] working on clay and they knew all the secrets of linear decoration. When [English poet] John Keats, writing in the first quarter of the nineteenth century, gazed at a Grecian urn, he was not primarily concerned with the red figures on a black ground, nor with the quality of the line drawings, nor yet with the difficulties attending a decorative scheme on a rounded surface. He was moved and inspired by the Greek feeling for the freshness of the world, and the calm, sacrificial joys of an artistic people. Thus he wrote, when observing the pictures on the urn.

> *Who are these coming to the sacrifice?*
> *To what green altar, O mysterious priest,*
> *Lead'st thou that heifer lowing at the skies,*
> *And all her silken flanks with garlands drest?*
> *What little town by river or sea shore,*
> *Or mountain-built with peaceful citadel,*
> *Is emptied of its folk, this pious morn?*
> *And, little town, thy streets for evermore*
> *Will silent be; and not a soul to tell*
> *Why thou art desolate, can e'er return.*

Increased Realism in Art, Literature, and Life

Michael Grant

Much has been written about Greek art, architecture, literature, philosophy, and science during the Classical Age (ca.500–323 B.C.) and for good reason, since the period produced many magnificent works in these fields. However, the age that followed— the Hellenistic (323–ca.30 B.C.)—in which Greek culture spread throughout the Near East, including Egypt, produced its own unique contributions to Greek culture, not only to the arts, but also to new social, literary, and religious outlooks on life, as well as the importance and rights of individual Greeks. First, Hellenistic times witnessed the emergence of a new preoccupation by both thinkers and ordinary people with the reality of the natural world. This stimulated more realistic artistic and literary depictions of men and women than had been seen in prior ages. At the same time, a new emphasis was placed on the individual and his or her feelings, needs, and desires (for the first time equal to that of the needs of the community). In this concise but fact-filled essay, University of Edinburgh scholar Michael Grant explores this new emphasis on realism and individuality. He first shows how the spirit of the age expanded educational opportunities and scientific inquiry, then explores the emphasis on the individual in literature (including the genres of biography, autobiography, and love poetry), sculpture, and painting (including realistic portrait busts).

A common form of education is one of the phenomena of the Hellenistic epoch. It was dominated by the rhetorical type of instruction advocated by the Athenian Isocrates (*d.*338), who had become the chief creator of rhetoric [the art of persuasive speaking] as a distinct science. For him, education above all

Michael Grant, *The Founders of the Western World: A History of Greece and Rome*. New York: Scribners, 1991. Copyright © 1991 by Michael Grant Publications, Ltd. Reproduced by permission of the publisher.

meant developing the ability *to speak*, which distinguishes human beings from animals—and was, in any case, the favourite occupation of the Greeks. Yet he was also at pains to propose a broader and more liberal programme than the mere rules and techniques of the professional rhetorician. In fact, he wanted to reduce theory to a minimum; whereas Aristotle on the other hand, although he saw the dangers of the rhetorical art, elaborated it by introducing a variety of new definitions. And it was under the influence of Aristotle's *Rhetoric* that Greek education assumed its typical Hellenistic form, characterized by a multitude of rhetorical textbooks.

In most parts of the Greek world the primary stages of teaching were left to private enterprise, although some cities appointed official supervisors of primary education (*paidonomoi*). Children were usually taught reading, writing, gymnastics and music, and sometimes painting, too. In secondary schools, physical and musical training proceeded further, and a certain amount of mathematics and science was taught as well. But literary subjects also played an extremely prominent part: Homer, Euripides and others were studied with care and in detail.

Athens, where this type of work was especially well developed, also became the model for the form of training known as the ephebate, organized in *c.*335 and 322, and copied at numerous other centres. It started as a sort of upper-class militia for eighteen-year-olds, but came to concentrate on character development and instruction in social behaviour. The ephebes congregated, and were taught, in their city's gymnasium, which increasingly superseded family life as the principal training ground of the young, and became, indeed, the focus and hallmark of Hellenism.

Directors of gymnasia, the gymnasiarchs, were appointed by their governments. But the extent of civic intervention varied widely from place to place. Rhodes and Miletus were among cities which believed that education should be the business of the state, as Plato and Aristotle had urged. Royal Pergamum had no less than five gymnasia. Like Rhodes and Athens, too, Pergamum was a place which provided a higher education, in rhetoric and philosophy. And in Alexandria was another centre where one could learn a variety of subjects at this more elevated level.

Seeing Things as They Are

Aristotle's share of responsibility for the rhetorical, word-orientated bias of Hellenistic education was counterbalanced by the stimulus that he also offered to Greek science. The scientific developments that continued to occur after his lifetime formed part of a new, general drive towards seeing things as they are: a drive, that is to say, towards greater reality and realism, accompanied by a conscious or unconscious jettisoning of some of the more idealistic, unreal conceptions that had characterized the classical past.

At the outset of this Hellenistic epoch, Aristotle's successor Theophrastus of Eresus on the island of Lesbos (*d.*288), while understandably dubious about the purposefulness (*telos*) of the universe envisaged by his master, nevertheless inherited his flair for classification, undertaking for botany what Aristotle had achieved for human beings and animals. After Theophrastus, the Greek study of biology did not advance much further. Other scientific studies, however, liberated at last from *a priori* speculations, showed greater progress than in any comparable period until the birth of modern science.

The same applied to mathematics, and one of the first men of learning to reside at Alexandria (*c.*300), where the Ptolemies lavishly stimulated such studies, was the mathematician Euclid. His summing up of the current condition of his subject was the culmination of all that had gone before, for the benefit of the future. His *Elements* demonstrated how knowledge can be attained by rational methods alone: and no book except the Bible has enjoyed such a long subsequent reign. Another Alexandrian, Ctesibius, who flourished in the 270s, was a versatile mechanical inventor. Then Strato of Lampsacus (*d.c.*269) confirmed the growing opinion that science had a right to exist independently of philosophy, and converted the Lyceum—of which he succeeded Theophrastus as head—from the latter to the former.

Archimedes of Syracuse (*d.*212) was a legendary mathematical genius who expanded the frontiers of knowledge. In solid geometry, he broke entirely new ground. He also prepared the way for the integral calculus, devised a new system for expressing large numbers, virtually invented hydrostatics, and excelled as an engineer. The polymath Eratosthenes of Cyrene (*c.*275–194), who lived at Athens and Alexandria, was the author of a *Geo-*

graphica, which was inspired by the conquests of Alexander the Great, and contributed to an accurate delineation of the surface of the earth. Greek mathematical geography was largely based on astronomy, which fascinated Hellenistic scholars. Aristarchus of Samos, a pupil of Strato, discovered that the earth revolves round the sun. Hipparchus of Nicaea (*c.*190–after 126) regarded this as unproven, but nevertheless transformed observational techniques, gaining recognition as the outstanding astronomer of antiquity.

Medicine, too, benefited from notable improvements. Most of the Hippocratic Corpus [writings of the famous Greek physician Hippocrates and his followers] was of Hellenistic date, and the various advances that its contents registered meant that the Greeks could now increasingly employ methods based not only on theory but on accumulated case studies as well. The dissections conducted by Herophilus of Calchedon, in the first half of the third century, enhanced knowledge of the brain, eye, duodenum, liver and reproductive organs. His younger colleague Erasistratus, who like him worked at Alexandria, made discoveries relating to digestion and the vascular (circulatory) system. Herophilus has been called the founder of anatomy, and Erasistratus of physiology. Moreover, Erasistratus also turned his attention to the nervous system, and led the way towards psychiatry. . . .

Realism in Literature

The impulse towards finding out about reality which had set science and medicine, for a time, on such a prominent course was paralleled in literature, and particularly in writings related to the operations of the human personality.

The thoughts of the Greeks had already been working in that direction when Euripides produced his harrowingly true-to-life personality studies, and when Aristotle amassed evidence about differing patterns of human behaviour. Then his pupil Theophrastus wrote his *Characters,* thirty satirical, razor-sharp sketches of persons suffering from various psychological flaws. One of his pupils was the Athenian practitioner of the New Comedy, Menander (*c.*342–292), who was also keenly interested in human emotions, at a down-to-earth level. Substantial passages or fragments of ten of his more than a hundred plays are now available, including a more or less complete text of the *Epitrepontes*

(Arbitrators). These works show that Menander prefers to avoid the politics dear to the Old Comedy of [the fifth-century B.C. Athenian playwright] Aristophanes, whose stock figures he replaces by more three-dimensional people. . . .

In the next generation, the literary mimes of Theocritus (c.300–260?)—who came from Syracuse, but lived at Cos and then worked mainly at Alexandria—introduced a new sort of realism. Mimetic dances had been popular since early times, and mime had now become the most favoured Greek theatrical form. For it was a popular medium among people who wanted a humorous, but direct and unencumbered, picture of the world around them. Theocritus, famous for his pastoral idylls . . . endowed this sort of composition with a new life, adapting the mime-form to elegant allusive verse, and employing his strong sense of the ridiculous to make fun of a vast section of contemporary life—the sort of men and women whom the poet's own fastidious circle despised. He brings to life their platitudinous [trite] sentiments with an unerring light touch, and the joke is enhanced by the inappropriately unnatural literary diction that he puts into the mouths of these trivial low-brow characters.

Not long afterwards Herodas, perhaps from Cos, evolved another type of literary mime, the *mimiambus*, comprising brief, pithy, versified sketches of relentless pungency. Once again part of the joke lies in the piquant contrast between his treatment of his themes, which is naturalistic and realistic, and the artificial, elevated, erudite style in which it is . . . framed.

Increased Realism in Art

The visual art of the Hellenistic period, while following on with direct continuity from the achievements of the previous epoch, nevertheless also rivalled contemporary literature in its increasedly determined move towards various forms of realism. The figure of the Apoxyomenus (Man Scraping Himself), made in the later years of the fourth century by Lysippus of Sicyon, shows not only a new and more natural, or at least more fashionable, set of anatomical proportions (smaller head, more slender body), but also a new sense of spiral movement, and a new three-dimensional method of composition. The Tyche (Fortune) of Antioch by his pupil Eutychides developed this three-dimensional concept further, presenting a cunning structure of lines and folds set obliquely in different planes.

The climax of these techniques, however, was to be seen in the no longer surviving bronze Helios or sun-god (Colossus) of Rhodes by another of Lysippus's pupils, the Rhodian Chares (292–280), and in the still extant [surviving] Victory (Nike) of Samothrace, by an unknown sculptor of early second-century BC. Originally tinted, the Victory is seen alighting exultantly upon a ship's prow—and a calculated counter-twist of her swirling, windswept robes shows how she is leaning forward to meet the rush of the wind.

Yet, somewhat paradoxically, this very time when drapery was receiving such sensitive attention also witnessed an intensification of the interest in the naked feminine form. . . . Thus the bodily planes of the Venus of Milo (Melos), of the second-century date, move and turn in multiple, contrasting directions, which reveal how, although classical purity and austerity have not been abandoned, they are modified by novel ideas and methods that have been mobilized to exploit the Hellenistic taste for realistic interpretation.

And meanwhile another sort of sculptural realism was developing too, with theatrical emphasis upon the emotions, which the sculptors of the time, echoing Aristotle, regarded as an essential element in human character. Major achievements in this field took place at Pergamum, the only royal capital where sculptors undertook extensive and important work with the backing of ample official patronage. Thus the bronze groups of statuary dedicated by the Pergamene king Attalus I Soter to the goddess Athena (c.200), in order to celebrate his victories over the Celtic Gauls (Galatians) who had invaded Asia Minor, was one of the most ambitious sculptural complexes ever attempted. The bronze originals have vanished, but a marble copy of the centrepiece still survives. It is the 'Ludovisi Group', consisting of the figure of a defeated, desperate Gaul stabbing himself to avoid capture while supporting the body of his wife whom he has just killed. Her limp, inanimate form contrasts with the tension of the man's contorted pose, as he plunges the dagger into his own neck. This central composition was originally surrounded by a series of half-recumbent figures, of which one, the 'Dying Gaul', is preserved, in the form of a fine copy, perhaps of the first century BC. . . .

For the 'Dying Gaul' once again combines the traditional simplifying pattern of Greek classicism with the emotional impact, and freshly direct observation of nature, which were features of contemporary Hellenistic art. There is emphasis upon the vanquished in this monument: they appear not as embodiments of evil, but in all the defiant agony of their defeat. And their portrayal is realistic. The same taste for realism, too, inspired other sculptors belonging to what has been called the 'miserabilistic' school, who depict hunchback dwarfs, and battered fishermen, and maudlin female alcoholics. And yet another facet of realism can be seen in the intimate, amusing terracotta statuettes which take their name from Tanagra in Boeotia, although they were first produced at Taras (Taranto, *c.*350) and then at Athens.

Wall-painting evidently reflected similar tendencies, represented above all by Apelles of Colophon (Değirmendere) in Ionia, who enjoyed the patronage of Alexander the Great and Ptolemy I Soter. His exploitation of illusionistic *trompe l'oeil* [a highly realistic painting style] and foreshortening effects was especially notable, and the men and women whom he painted were shown exhibiting a whole range of different emotions. He specialized in easel-paintings, none of which have survived.

But his style may well be reflected in some of the large pebble-mosaics of the period. One such mosaic at Pella, the capital of Macedonia, is a picture of a stag-hunt signed by Gnosis (*c.*320–300), whose foreshortened figures and shaded, wind-blown draperies convey an illusion of depth and of real life, as it appears to the eye.

Rise of Individualism

This realism was a keynote of contemporary art, because it mirrored what Hellenistic man was thinking and feeling. And, by the same token, he was individualistic. Despite all the troubles of the time, he was liberated from many earlier conventions and restraints, and more and more conscious of his own capacities and needs and rights. City-state life had weakened, and the royal centres were too remote to occupy its place. To fill the vacuum, people belonged to clubs, lived in better houses, read more—and read about other individuals.

Theophrastus's *Characters* had described what individuals were like, without naming anybody in particular. But people also wanted to read about real, important, picturesque men—in an age which indulged, freely, in personality cult. They were catered for by Aristoxenus of Taras (*b*.375/360), who did much to develop, out of earlier precedents, the art of biography—including lives not only of men of action, but of philosophers as well. In the third century, Satyrus of Callatis Pontica (Mangalia) composed further biographies, writing attractively but inserting much legendary material. But the *Lives of Philosophers* by Antigonus of Carystus (*c*.240) showed an unprecedentedly high standard of accurate description. So biography, by now, had been launched; and autobiography, too, was foreshadowed by the *Memoirs* of the Achaean League statesman Aratus of Sicyon.

Sculptural portraiture, the visual counterpart of the biographer's art, was likewise virtually an original creation of the Hellenistic world. Men who sought to depict Alexander the Great set the tone. The king's own favourite sculptor, as far as portraits of himself were concerned, was Lysippus of Sicyon, who alone, Alexander believed, could truly capture the leonine aspect of his appearance. Such portraits, like other forms of art, retained a delicate balance between the old idealism and the new realistic trends: as Lysippus himself remarked, 'While others made men as they were, I make them as they appeared to be'—or as they wanted to be, for heads of early Hellenistic monarchs tend not only to reproduce their actual features, but also to hint at the providential foresight and care for his subjects that a king ought to display, and wished to seem to be displaying.

A New View of Women and Love

So realism, of a sort, was a characteristic of 'Hellenistic man'. But this was also an age when Greek women came to the fore. As we saw, Hellenistic sculptors, for the first time, were exploring the naked bodies of women: and this was only one aspect of a whole phenomenon of female emergence that was typical of the age.

The tendency was stimulated by the careers of queens of terrifying ability and force, enjoying unlimited freedom of action and power: women such as Arsinoe II Philadelphus, sister and wife of Ptolemy II of Egypt. The reverence accorded to these

Ptolemaic queens was related to the worship of the mother-goddess Isis, with whom, indeed, it seemed natural that such formidable human women should be identified.

But, in addition, the prestige and activities of such personages could not fail to contribute to the emancipation of women in general—which in consequence proceeded on a substantial scale, though sometimes patchily. Liberation had at least gone far enough for two ladies whom Theocritus brings to the festival of Adonis to grumble about their husbands in a highly unsubservient fashion. . . .

The development of private houses made women's lives more agreeable, and eminent women of the time included a portrait-painter, an architect, harpists and at least three poets.

And male poets, too, wrote elegies and epigrams reflecting a new kind of literary interest in the analysis of heterosexual love. The best epigrams of Asclepiades of Samos (c.290), for example, deal with this kind of erotic theme, employing his original, dramatic talent to explore the neurotic obsessions which accompanied it. But love, to him, meant sex more than romance. The women he wrote about were mostly attractive prostitutes (hetairai), and he commented on them in satirical and scandalous language—himself being weary of living, to use his own words, at the age of scarcely twenty-two. Theocritus, too, agrees with him in failing to envisage love as an ennobling or purifying passion, but stresses it for a different reason: because he knows all about the misery of amorous frustration, the agony of the heart.

In the next generation Apollonius Rhodius, librarian at Alexandria from c.260 to c.247, by depicting Medea's passion for Jason in his poem the *Argonautica*, became the first poet to use love, romantic love, as the central theme of a whole epic. And meanwhile the same passion, too, of a more middle-brow and saccharine nature, was the main feature of a series of Greek novels that were being launched on the world, perhaps under Egyptian influence, and were supplemented, subsequently, by spicier short stories, the *Milesian Tales*.

Advances in Medical Science

Philip Wheelwright

A major burst of Greek philosophic-scientific inquiry in the fifth and fourth centuries B.C. helped to spur the rise of the most scientifically based and practical medical institution history had yet seen. In particular, the members of the medical school founded by Hippocrates of Cos attempted to understand the physical realities of health and disease. The Hippocratic notion that health and disease have natural causes and can be manipulated by human intervention marked a giant step away from supernatural explanations, which had been (and remained) common, and toward a rational scientific approach. In this essay, Philip Wheelwright, formerly of the University of California, Riverside, discusses the main Hippocratic ideas and methods.

The most considerable body of medical writings that has come down from ancient Greece is that associated with the name of Hippocrates (460–390 B.C.). On his native island of Cos Hippocrates founded what was probably the first school of medicine dedicated unflinchingly to the investigation and application of scientific principles. The extant writings of that school constitute what is called the Hippocratic Corpus; although their individual authorship is undiscoverable in most cases, they are apparently typical expressions of the methods employed by that school of physicians and of their resulting speculations. At any rate, for convenience and by accepted custom, we shall use the name of Hippocrates when referring to the authors of the excerpts.

Although Hippocrates never organized the philosophical principles of his thinking, and although it is impossible to be sure how much of the Corpus was written by the master himself and how much by medical disciples, we can best think of his philosophy as resting upon a pair of complementary propositions: (a)

Philip Wheelwright, *The Presocratics*. New York: Macmillan, 1966. Copyright © 1966 by The Macmillan Publishing Company. Reproduced by permission.

Health is the natural state, disease is unnatural; and (b) *Disease, no less than health, is governed by natural causes*, which it is the task of the physician to understand. Are these two propositions contradictory? In discovering the sense in which they are consistent from Hippocrates' point of view, and are to him equally important sides of the truth about human organisms, we take an important step into an understanding of his philosophy.

To describe health as "natural" has for Hippocrates a very specific meaning. Living nature is telic [purposeful], it moves toward certain discoverable biological goals. Referring to the cycle of births and deaths which marks the career of every living species Hippocrates postulates that each organism tends by nature to play its part in that cycle in a healthy manner, appropriately to the species of which it is a member, unless something hinders. When a creature is injured or falls ill, provided that its departure from normal is not unduly severe, it tends by the force of its own living nature to heal the injured part and to restore the balance that is health. Since this is so, the role of the physician as Hippocrates conceives it is not to manipulate the patient as one would handle something inanimate, but to remove, both from within and from outside the patient's body, obstructions to healthy recovery. The essential relation is not dyadic [two-fold], he holds, but triadic [three-fold]: the physician, the patient, and the disease.

A Doctor's Job

But if there is one sense in which health is the natural state, there is also a sense in which disease likewise is a part of nature. For the possibility of understanding disease lies, Hippocrates insists, in the fact that disease is not entirely haphazard, however it may appear superficially, but follows patterns of development which in general, if not always in detail, can be traced. What, then, is the physician's task with respect to it? Hippocrates defines that task in terms of arranging the bodily and environmental conditions so that the disease can go through its own peculiar cycle as expeditiously and safely as possible. Proper food and drink, calmness of mind and body, suitable exercise, and the like, are among the chief ways in which the bodily conditions can be made as favorable as possible to the speedy and firm completion of the cycle through illness and back again to health.

When illness begins it is marked by an excess of some bodily element over the rest—say an excess of heat, as in a fever, or of moisture as in dropsy. This excessive element is an intruder and a usurper: it must be either expelled or sent back to its proper place in the bodily complex. The physical body contains within

A Doctor's Oath

This oath, attributed to Hippocrates, is still memorized and adhered to by modern physicians.

I swear by Apollo the physician, and Aesculapius, and Health, and All-heal, and all the gods and goddesses, that, according to my ability and judgment, I will keep this Oath and this stipulation—to reckon him who taught me this Art equally dear to me as my parents, to share my substance with him, and relieve his necessities if required; to look upon his offspring in the same footing as my own brothers, and to teach them this art, if they shall wish to learn it, without fee or stipulation; and that by precept, lecture, and every other mode of instruction, I will impart a knowledge of the Art to my own sons, and those of my teachers, and to disciples bound by a stipulation and oath according to the law of medicine, but to none others. I will follow that system of regimen which, according to my ability and judgment, I consider for the benefit of my patients, and abstain from whatever is deleterious and mischievous. I will give no deadly medicine to any one if asked, nor suggest any such counsel; and in like manner I will not give to a woman a pessary to produce abortion. With purity and with holiness I will pass my life and practice my Art. I will not cut persons laboring under the stone, but will leave this to be done by men who are practitioners of this work. Into whatever houses I enter, I will go into them for the benefit of the sick, and will abstain from every voluntary act of mischief and corruption; and, further, from the seduction of females or males, of freemen and slaves. Whatever, in connection with my professional practice or not, in connection with it, I see or hear, in the life of men, which ought not to be spoken of abroad, I will not divulge, as reckoning that all such should be kept secret. While I continue to keep this Oath unviolated, may it be granted to me to enjoy life and the practice of the art, respected by all men, in all times! But should I trespass and violate this Oath, may the reverse be my lot!

Quoted in Kenneth J. Atchity, ed., *The Classical Greek Reader.* New York: Oxford University Press, 1996, p. 153.

itself the forces of healing, which act generally by a process called *pepsis*, which can be translated both as coction or cooking and as digestion. The physician must learn its character and role with respect to the particular patient and disease with which he is concerned. The wise physician will know when to try to aid and accelerate the peptic process and when to let it alone. The situation differs in different organisms; the physician cannot work by strict rule, but must watch for the "opportune moment" (*kairos*) when the situation is exactly right for the exercise of his art. There comes at some point the "crisis" (*krisis*), the moment at which the balance is ready to be tipped either way—so that the patient succumbs to the disproportionate mixture or so that the healthy forces begin to regain their ascendancy and the patient begins to recover. Since health was regarded as a right proportion of the elements in the organic body, and any ailment or disease as a disproportion, it was logical to regard the *krisis* as somehow marking a change, or the beginning of a change, from disproportion to proportion. Such a change involves, by Greek medical logic, a "washing away" (*katharsis, katharmos*) of the superfluous elements that caused the disproportion and the reestablishment of the new "blended maturity" (*krasis*) which is health.

What Caused Illness?

But what precisely is it that by becoming excessive or defective produces variations of health? What is it that gets washed away, catharated, as a step in the curing of illness, or gets built up by proper regimen? To ask this question is to ask, in Aristotle's later terminology, about the nature of the "material cause." What are the material factors, the bodily ingredients, whose right proportion constitutes health? The Pythagorean physicians at Crotona conceived such ingredients in terms of pairs of contrary qualities, explaining health accordingly as a right proportion and blend of moisture and dryness, of cold and heat, etc., in the body. The physicians who were influenced by Empedocles, in the so-called Sicilian school of medicine, conceived their problem in terms of the four basic substances: too much earth in the human body and psyche was taken to be the cause both of constipation and of general lethargy, too much water as causing either catarrhal [inflammation and discharge from the nose and throat] and other discharges or in extreme cases dropsy [swelling caused by an accumulation of fluids], too much fire as causing both bodily fever and ecstatic mental genius [The fourth basic substance was air.]. Hippocrates criticized both of these medical groups for making assumptions which could not be sufficiently tested and for seeking their explanations in areas too remote from the perceptible facts of bodily life. What we actually find within the body, he said, are "flowing juices"; which he classified (on the basis of such physiological observations as it was then possible to make) as blood, yellow bile, black bile, and phlegm. The Greek word for flowing juice was *chymos,* which later got taken into the Latin language as *"humor,"* and the subsequent "doctrine of humors" in European medical theory had a long and quaint history. But the Greek word in Hippocrates' time meant simply "that which flows"; and the doctrine as he and his followers developed it represents in essence a first step toward a science of physiological chemistry.

Chronology

B.C.

ca. 3000–ca. 1100

Greece experiences its Bronze Age, in which people use tools and weapons made of bronze.

ca. 2000

Tribal peoples speaking an early form of Greek begin entering the Greek peninsula from the east or northeast; their descendants, whom scholars refer to as Mycenaeans, spread across mainland Greece.

ca. 1500–ca. 1400

Mycenaean warlords overthrow another early Aegean people, the Minoans, who have long controlled Crete.

ca. 1200–ca. 1100

For reasons still unclear, the Mycenaean kingdoms and fortresses suffer widespread destruction and rapidly decline.

ca. 1100–ca. 800

Greece's Dark Age, in which poverty and illiteracy are at first widespread and about which modern scholars know very little.

ca. 850–750

The most likely period in which the legendary epic poet Homer lived and composed the *Iliad* and the *Odyssey*.

ca. 800–ca. 500

Greece's Archaic Age, characterized by the rise of city-states, the return of prosperity and literacy, rapid population growth, and intensive colonization of the Mediterranean and Black Seas.

776

The traditional date for the first Olympic Games, held at Olympia, in the northwestern Peloponnesus.

594

The Athenians make a leading citizen named Solon archon (administrator), charging him with the task of revising Athens's social and political system.

ca. 559

Cyrus II, "the Great," founds the Persian Empire (centered in what is now Iran), whose rulers, interests, and conquests will consistently affect Greek history and affairs.

508

Building on Solon's reforms, an aristocrat named Cleisthenes and his supporters transform Athens's government into the world's first democracy.

ca. 500–323

Greece's Classical Age, in which Greek arts, architecture, literature, and democratic reforms reach their height.

490

The Persian ruler Darius sends an expedition to sack Athens, but the Athenians decisively defeat the invaders at Marathon, northeast of Athens.

480

Darius's son, Xerxes, launches a massive invasion of Greece; the Greeks win a series of stunning victories and in the following year expel the Persians from the Aegean sphere.

461

In Athens, a leading democratic politician named Pericles becomes the city's most influential leader.

447

Construction begins on a major new temple complex atop Athens's Acropolis; nine years later, the magnificent Parthenon temple is dedicated to the goddess Athena.

431

Sparta declares war on Athens, initiating the disastrous Peloponnesian War, which engulfs and exhausts almost all the city-states.

404

Athens surrenders, ending the great war and initiating a Spartan hegemony (domination) of Greece.

371

The Theban leader Epaminondas defeats the Spartans at Leuctra (near Thebes), and soon afterward invades the Peloponnesus, initiating a period of Theban hegemony.

359

King Philip II takes charge of disunited, culturally backward Macedonia and soon begins to forge Europe's first national standing army.

338

Philip and his teenaged son, Alexander (who will later be called "the Great"), defeat an alliance of city-states at Chaeronea (in western Boeotia).

334–323

After Philip's assassination, Alexander invades Persia, carves out the largest empire the world has yet seen, and dies in the Persian capital of Babylon.

323–30

Greece's Hellenistic Age, in which Alexander's generals, the so-called successors, war among themselves and carve up his empire into several new kingdoms, which then proceed also to fight among themselves; during the second half of this period, Rome gains control of the Greek world.

ca. 280

Three large Greek monarchies (the Macedonian, Seleucid, and Ptolemaic kingdoms) have by now emerged from the chaos of the long wars of the successors.

200–197

Rome prosecutes and wins the Second Macedonian War against Macedonia's King Philip V.

171–168

Rome wins the Third Macedonian War against Philip's son, Perseus and dismantles the Macedonian kingdom.

146

A Roman general destroys the once-great Greek city of Corinth as an object lesson to any Greeks contemplating rebellion against Rome.

31

The Roman leader Octavian (the future emperor Augustus) defeats the Roman general Mark Antony and Greek queen of Egypt, Cleopatra, at Actium, in western Greece; the following year, the legendary queen, last of the Hellenistic and major autonomous Greek rulers of antiquity, takes her own life.

For Further Research

Ancient Sources in Translation

Aristotle, *Politics*, in *The Philosophy of Aristotle*. Ed. Renford Bambrough. New York: New American Library, 1963.

Kenneth J. Atchity, ed., *The Classical Greek Reader*. New York: Oxford University Press, 1996.

Hesiod, *Theogony*, in *Classical Gods and Heroes: Myths as Told by the Ancient Authors*. Ed. and trans. Rhoda A. Hendricks. New York: Morrow Quill, 1974.

Lysias, *On the Killing of Eratosthenes the Seducer*, in *The Murder of Herodes and Other Trials from the Athenian Law Courts*, by Kathleen Freeman. New York: W.W. Norton, 1963.

Pindar, *Odes*. Trans. C.M. Bowra. New York: Penguin, 1969.

Sophocles, *Oedipus the King*. Trans. Bernard M.W. Knox. New York: Pocket Books, 1959.

Thucydides, *The Peloponnesian War*. Trans. Rex Warner. New York: Penguin, 1972.

Xenophon, *Oeconomicus* (or *The Estate Manager*), in *Xenophon: Conversations with Socrates*. Trans. Hugh Tredennick and Robin Waterfield. New York: Penguin, 1990.

Modern Sources

Art, Architecture, Philosophy, and Science

Manolis Andronicos, *The Acropolis*. Athens: Ekdotike Athenon, 1994.

Carl Bluemel, *Greek Sculptors at Work*. London: Phaidon, 1969.

John Boardman, *The Parthenon and Its Sculptures*. Austin: University of Texas Press, 1985.

———, ed., *The Oxford History of Classical Art*. Oxford, England: Oxford University Press, 1993.

C.M. Bowra, *Ancient Greek Literature*. New York: Oxford University Press, 1960.

J.J. Coulton, *Ancient Greek Architects at Work*. Ithaca, NY: Cornell University Press, 1977.

Thomas Craven, *The Pocket Book of Greek Art*. New York: Pocket Books, 1950.

Peter Green, *The Parthenon*. New York: Newsweek Book Division, 1973.

R.M. Hare, *Plato*. New York: Oxford University Press, 1982.

A.W. Lawrence, *Greek Architecture*. New Haven, CT: Yale University Press, 1996.

David C. Lindberg, *The Beginnings of Western Science*. Chicago: University of Chicago Press, 1992.

Don Nardo, *The Parthenon*. San Diego: Lucent Books, 1999.

———, *Greek and Roman Science*. San Diego: Lucent Books, 1997.

J.J. Pollitt, *Art in the Hellenistic Age*. Cambridge, England: Cambridge University Press, 1986.

Nigel Spivey, *Greek Art*. London: Phaidon, 1997.

A.E. Taylor, *Socrates: The Man and His Thought*. New York: Doubleday, 1952.

Rex Warner, *The Greek Philosophers*. New York: New American Library, 1958.

Philip Wheelwright, ed., *The Presocratics*. New York: Macmillan, 1966.

R.E. Wycherly, *The Stones of Athens*. Princeton, NJ: Princeton University Press, 1978.

Democracy, Citizenship, and Legal Institutions

R.A. Bauman, *Political Trials in Ancient Greece*. New York: Routledge, 1990.

David Cohen, *Law, Violence, and Community in Classical Athens*. New York: Cambridge University Press, 1995.

J.K. Davies, *Democracy and Classical Greece*. Cambridge, MA: Harvard University Press, 1993.

Donald Kagan, *Pericles of Athens and the Birth of Democracy*. New York: Free, 1991.

Don Nardo, *The Trial of Socrates*. San Diego: Lucent Books, 1997.

Alfred Zimmern, *The Greek Commonwealth: Politics and Economics in Fifth-Century Athens*. 1931. Reprint, New York: Oxford University Press, 1961.

Family, Women, Slaves, and Social Life

Sue Blundell, *Women in Ancient Greece*. Cambridge, MA: Harvard University Press, 1995.

Andrew Dalby, *Siren Feasts: A History of Food and Gastronomy in Greece*. New York: Routledge, 1996.

N.R.E. Fisher, *Slavery in Classical Greece*. London: Bristol Classical, 1993.

————, *Social Values in Classical Athens*. London: Dent, 1976.

Frank J. Frost, *Greek Society*. Lexington, MA: D.C. Heath, 1980.

Mark Golden, *Children and Childhood in Classical Athens*. Baltimore: Johns Hopkins University Press, 1990.

Michael Grant, *A Social History of Greece and Rome*. New York: Scribner's, 1992.

Don Nardo, *Women of Ancient Greece*. San Diego: Lucent Books, 2000.

Sarah B. Pomeroy, *Goddesses, Whores, Wives, and Slaves: Women in Classical Antiquity*. New York: Shocken Books, 1995.

General Ancient Greek History and Culture

Lesley Adkins and Roy A. Adkins, *Handbook to Life in Ancient Greece*. New York: Facts On File, 1997.

C.M. Bowra, *Classical Greece*. New York: Time-Life, 1965.

————, *The Greek Experience*. New York: New American Library, 1957.

Lionel Casson, *The Ancient Mariners*. New York: Macmillan, 1959.

Charles Freeman, *Egypt, Greece, and Rome: Civilizations of the Ancient Mediterranean*. New York: Oxford University Press, 1996.

————, *The Greek Achievement: The Foundation of the Western World*. New York: Viking/Penguin, 1999.

Michael Grant, *The Founders of the Western World: A History of Greece and Rome*. New York: Scribner's, 1991.

————, *The Rise of the Greeks*. New York: Macmillan, 1987.

W.G. Hardy, *The Greek and Roman World*. Cambridge, MA: Schenkman, 1962.

Joint Association of Classical Teachers, *The World of Athens*. New York: Cambridge University Press, 1984.

Robert B. Kebric, *Greek People*. Mountain View, CA: Mayfield, 1997.

Peter Levi, *Atlas of the Greek World*. New York: Facts On File, 1984.

Thomas R. Martin, *Ancient Greece: From Prehistoric to Hellenistic Times*. New Haven, CT: Yale University Press, 1996.

Christian Meier, *Athens: Portrait of a City in Its Golden Age*. Trans. Robert and Rita Kimber. New York: Henry Holt, 1998.

Don Nardo, *The History of Weapons and Warfare: Ancient Greece*. San Diego: Lucent Books, 2003.

———, *Life in Ancient Athens*. San Diego: Lucent Books, 2000.

———, *The Decline and Fall of Ancient Greece*. San Diego: Greenhaven, 2000.

Sarah B. Pomeroy et al., *Ancient Greece: A Political, Social, and Cultural History*. New York: Oxford University Press, 1999.

C.E. Robinson, *Everyday Life in Ancient Greece*. Oxford, England: Clarendon, 1968.

Chester G. Starr, *The Ancient Greeks*. New York: Oxford University Press, 1971.

———, *A History of the Ancient World*. New York: Oxford University Press, 1991.

George D. Wilcoxon, *Athens Ascendant*. Ames: Iowa State University Press, 1979.

Religion

Manolis Andronicos, *Delphi*. Athens: Ekdotiki Athenon, 1993.

David Bellingham, *An Introduction to Greek Mythology*. Secaucus, NJ: Chartwell Books, 1989.

Robert Garland, *The Greek Way of Death*. Ithaca, NY: Cornell University Press, 1985.

Michael Grant, *Myths of the Greeks and Romans*. New York: Penguin, 1962.

Edith Hamilton, *Mythology*. New York: New American Library, 1940.

Donna C. Kurtz and John Boardman, *Greek Burial Customs*. Ithaca: Cornell University Press, 1971.

John D. Mikalson, *Athenian Popular Religion*. Chapel Hill: University of North Carolina Press, 1983.

Don Nardo, *The Greenhaven Encyclopedia of Greek and Roman Mythology*. San Diego: Greenhaven, 2002.

Jennifer Neils, *Goddess and Polis: The Panathenaic Festival in Ancient Athens*. Princeton, NJ: Princeton University Press, 1992.

Sports and Games

M.I. Finley and H.W. Pleket, *The Olympic Games: The First Thousand Years*. New York: Viking, 1976.

Don Nardo, *Greek and Roman Sport*. San Diego: Lucent Books, 1999.

Vera Olivova, *Sports and Games in the Ancient World*. New York: St. Martin's, 1984.

Michael B. Poliakoff, *Combat Sports in the Ancient World*. New Haven, CT: Yale University Press, 1987.

Judith Swaddling, *The Ancient Olympic Games*. Austin: University of Texas Press, 1980, 1996.

David C. Young, *The Olympic Myth of Greek Amateur Athletics*. Chicago: Ares, 1984.

Theater and Drama

Iris Brooke, *Costume in Greek Classic Drama*. London: Methuen, 1962.

James H. Butler, *The Theater and Drama of Greece and Rome*. San Francisco: Chandler, 1972.

John Ferguson, *A Companion to Greek Tragedy*. Austin: University of Texas Press, 1972.

Don Nardo, *Ancient Greek Drama*. San Diego: Greenhaven, 2000.

———, ed., *Readings on Antigone*. San Diego: Greenhaven, 2000.

———, ed., *Readings on Sophocles*. San Diego: Greenhaven, 1997.

———, ed., *Greek and Roman Theater*. San Diego: Lucent Books, 1995.

T.B.L. Webster, *Greek Theater Production*. London: Methuen, 1970.

Index

Acharnians (Aristophanes), 79
Acropolis, 10–12, 29, 103, 106
  temple complex on Athens
    hilltop, 102
  see also Parthenon
adultery
  case of, 70–74
  laws against, 75–77
Aeschylus, 15
Aesop, 27
Agora, 85
Alexander the Great, 122, 123
Alexandria, 117, 118, 119
Alkimidas, 97
Alpheios, 92, 99
Altis, 91–94, 99
  Olympic races designed to finish
    at, 95–96
amphora (pottery), 111, 113
Anaximander, 14
*Ancient Greece: From Prehistoric to
  Hellenistic Times* (Martin), 65
Ancient Mariners, The (Casson),
  86–87
animals, 51
  classification of, 15
  sacrifice of, 12
Antigonus, 123
Antiochus IV Epiphanes, 33
Apelles, 122
Aphrodite (dcity), 63
Apollonius Rhodius, 124
Archimedes of Syracuse, 102, 118
architecture, 10, 11, 49, 102
  see also Parthenon
Argonautica (Appollonius
  Rhodius), 124
Aristarchus of Samos, 119
Aristeides, 54
Aristophanes, 15, 54, 56, 80–81
  attitude of, toward slaves, 30
  attitude of, toward Socrates and
    sophism, 57
  comic heroes of, 79, 122

Aristotle, 14, 15, 24, 89, 102
  beginnings of realism and, 119
  influence of, on education, 117,
    118
  Lyceum of, 20
  on slavery, 26, 28, 32
Aristoxenus, 123
Arsinoe II Philadelphus, 123
art, 102, 112
  clothing depicted in, 44
  increased realism in, 120–21
  individualism in, 122–23
  murals, 113, 122
  portrayal of dining customs in,
    48–49
  see also pottery
artisans, 84–88, 99, 103, 106,
  111–12
Assembly of Athens, 56, 78,
  82–83, 107
  opening of, 79–81
Atchity, Kenneth J., 127
Athena, 11, 45
  artistic representations of, 114,
    121
  statue of, at Parthenon, 12, 103,
    104–105, 108–109
Athens, 11, 24, 50, 57
  education in, 14, 20
  first democracy in, 60
  mass production of pottery in,
    112
  number of slaves in, 26, 27
  strangers encouraged to settle
    in, 88
  wealth of, 89–90
  work in, 84–87, 105–107
  see also Assembly of Athens
Athens in the Age of Pericles
  (Robinson), 80
athletics, 10, 23
  as part of general education, 24,
    53, 54–55, 117
  Spartan emphasis on, 18, 21

see also Olympic Games
Atlas, 68
Attalus I Soter (king of Pergamum), 121
Augeas (king of Elis), 93

Bambrough, R., 28
banking, 60, 87, 88–89
Bowra, C.M., 97
Briareus, 62, 65, 68, 69
  in war against Titans, 66–67
Brooke, Iris, 42

Capture of Troy (Polygnotus), 114
Casson, Lionel, 86–87
Characters (Theophrastus), 119, 123
children, 19–20, 47
chiton (tunic), 42–45
chlamys (short cloak), 46
chorus, 16, 54, 81
Classical Greek Reader, The (Atchity), 127
clothing, 23, 45–46
  Doric style, 42–43
  Ionic style, 43–44
Clouds (Aristophanes), 57
Constitution of the Athenians (Dakyns), 80
Cottus, 62, 65, 68, 69
  in war against Titans, 66–67
crater (pottery), 111
Craven, Thomas, 110
creation stories, 61–65
Crete, 64, 110
Cronus, 62–64
  landmark hill at Olympia named for, 92, 95
Ctesibius, 118
Cyclopes, 62

Dakyns, H.G., 80
Dalby, Andrew, 47
dancing, 20, 50, 54
deities, 12, 15, 60, 68–69
  artistic depictions of, 113–14
  creation of, 61–65
  festivals and games held in honor of, 54, 55, 92–95

war between, 66–67
  see also Aphrodite; Athena; Dionysus; Uranus; Zeus
Delos, 26, 50
democracy, 17, 29, 56, 78, 80
  contrast between ancient and modern, 82–83
  necessity for literacy and, 53
Democritus, 14, 102
Demosthenes, 78–79, 82
Dionysus, 54
  artistic representations of, 114
  deity of theatrical production, 15
dolphins, 51
drama. *See* theater
Dying Gaul (sculpture), 121–22

education, 20–21, 23, 57–58, 116–18
  minimal role of women in, 24
  music in, 54
  physical training in, 55
  private, 53
  public lectures and, 13
  separation of ethics and science and, 14–15
  sophism and, 56
Egypt, 33
Elements (Euclid), 118
Elis, 50, 94
  training for Olympic Games held at, 98–99
Empedocles, 128
ephebate (youth training), 117
Epictetus, 92
Epicurus, 102
Erasistratus, 119
Eratosthenes, 118
Erechtheum, 86, 87
Euclid, 118
Euripides, 15, 30, 79, 117
Eutychides, 120–21

fertility rites, 95
food, 47, 50–52
Funeral Speech (Pericles), 90

Gaea (earth goddess), 61, 64

children of, 62
revenge of, against Uranus, 63
Games at Nemea, 94
Geographica (Eratosthenes),
  118–19
Grant, Michael, 25, 116
Green, Peter, 103
Guide to Greece (Levi), 114
Gyges, 62, 65, 68–69

Hades, 69
Hardy, W.G., 84
Helios of Rhodes (sculpture), 121
Hellanodikai (Olympic Games
  officials), 97–98, 99, 100
Hendricks, Rhoda A., 61
Hephaesteion, 86
Heracles, 114
Herodas, 120
Herodotus, 30, 50, 51, 102
Herophilus, 119
Hesiod, 27, 60
himation (cloak), 45–46
Hipparchus, 119
Hippocrates, 102, 119, 125–26,
  129
  Hippocratic oath and, 127
Histories (Herodotus), 50
Homer, 20, 43, 54, 60, 117
houses, 124
  dining rooms and, 48–49

Iktinos, 103
Iliad (Homer), 54
industries, 60, 84–85, 88
  slaves and, 27, 29
Iphitos (king of Elis), 93–94, 98
Isocrates, 57–58, 116–17
Isthmian Games, 94

Joint Association of Classical
  Teachers, 53

Kagan, Donald, 78
katharsis, 128
Keats, John, 115
Knox, Bernard M.W., 16

laws, 60, 77

against adultery, 75–76
on slavery, 26, 32, 33
of Sparta, 49–50
see also legal case
Laws (Plato), 32, 49–50
legal case, 70, 71
  arguments in, 75–76
  epilogue in, 77
  narrative on adulterous
    situation in, 72–74
Levi, Peter, 114
literature, 124
  biography and, 123
  in education, 24, 117
  realism in, 119–20
  slavery portrayed in, 27
  see also poetry
liturgies (taxes), 88, 90
Lives of Philosophers (Antigonus),
  123
Ludovisi Group (sculpture), 121
Lyceum, 20, 118
Lysias, 29, 70
Lysippus, 120–21, 123

marriage, 36–37, 71–72
  division of labor in, 38–41
  unrecognized between slaves, 26
Martin, Thomas R., 65
masks, 16
mathematics, 14, 117, 118
meat, 51, 52
medicine. *See* science, medical
Memoirs (Aratus), 123
men
  entertainment of guests by,
    47–48
  Spartan rules for, 19, 20
Menander, 26, 33, 119–20
Meno (Plato), 15
metics (resident aliens), 85, 88,
  90
Miletus, 50, 117
mime form, 120
mosaics, 122
music, 55
  as part of education, 20, 24, 117
  as part of religious festivals, 50,
    54

Odyssey (Homer), 27, 42, 43, 44, 54
Oeconomica (Pseudo-Aristotle), 32
Oeconomicus (Xenophon), 35
Olympia, 60, 92, 109
  influx of visitors for Games at, 99
  length of track at, 96
  statue of Zeus at, 93
Olympic Games, 10, 60, 91, 99–100
  athletes honored at, 97
  construction of stadium and, 95–96
  origins of, 93–94
  setting for, 92
  training for, 98
Olympic Truce, 94
Olympus, 66
On the Crown (Demosthenes), 82
Oracle, 94

Panathenaic festival, 103, 108
Panathenaic Games, 55, 113
Parthenon, 11, 86, 103
  construction of, 107
  design of, 104
  materials for, 11, 105–106
  ornamentation of, 108
  scandal of Phidias's statue and, 109
Pausanias, 114
peplos (tunic), 46
Peloponnesian War, 29, 84, 86, 90
Pelops, 93
Pentelicus marble, 105
Pergamum, 117
Pericles, 78, 82, 88, 90
  construction of Parthenon and, 11, 103, 104, 107, 109
Persephone, 69
Phidias, 93, 102–104, 107–109
Philip II (king of Macedonia), 33, 82, 86
philosophy, 13–15, 55–58, 102
Philosophy of Aristotle, The (Bambrough), 28
Pindar, 93, 97

Pindar: Odes (Bowra), 97
Plato, 35, 102
  academies founded by, 14, 20, 24, 55
  admiration of, for Spartan discipline, 49–50
  attitude of, toward slavery, 26, 32
  attitude of, toward sophism, 56, 57
  on education, 54, 117
  scientific research and, 15
Plutarch, 11, 19, 106
Pnyx, 78, 79, 82
poetry, 20, 54, 55, 124
Politics (Aristotle), 28, 85
Polygnotus, 113, 114
Poseidon, 64, 68, 69, 94
pottery, 88, 102, 110
  competitive market for, 85
  decoration of, 114–15
    black figure style in, 111
  practicality of, 112–13
  slaves among the creators of, 29
Protagoras of Abdera, 57
Pseudo-Aristotle, 32
Ptolemy I Soter, 122
Pythagoras, 14, 51, 102

religion, 10, 47, 65
  festivals and, 50, 60, 113
  prayer and, 12–13
  as subject of art, 113–14
Republic (Plato), 88
Rhea, 63
  children of, 64
rhetoric, 20, 56, 116–18
  standard elements of,
    demonstrated in legal case, 70
    Arguments, 75–77
    Epilogue, 77
    Narrative, 71–75
    Proem, 71
Rhetoric (Aristotle), 117
Rhodes, 117
Robinson, C.A., 80

sailing, 89
science, 13–15, 119

medical, 102, 125–29
silver mines, 27, 88
Sixth Nemean Ode (Pindar), 97
slavery, 23
    effects of, on labor and industry,
        27
    Greek and Roman civilizations
        facilitated by, 25
    increase in, 28–29
    rationalization for, 30–34
    see also slaves
slaves, 10, 33, 47, 79
    Athenian laws to protect, 30
    comments of various writers on,
        31–32
    exclusion of, from theatrical
        productions, 17
    industry and, 85, 86
    numbers and status of, 26–29
    in silver mines, 27, 88
social customs, 10, 60
    related to dining, 47–50
    see also marriage; religion;
        slavery
Socrates, 35, 57, 86, 102
    separation between philosophy
        and science and, 14–15
    as stonemason, 85
sophists, 20, 55–57
Sophocles, 15
Sparta, 23, 49, 53, 88
    dining customs of, 50
    educational system of, 20–21, 55
    role of women in, 18–19
stoics, 33–34
Strato, 118, 119
Styx, 69
Swaddling, Judith, 91

Tartarus, 68–69
taxes, 88, 90
temples, 12–13, 86, 102, 104, 113
    shrines and, 42, 48
    Temple of Hera, 94
    see also Acropolis
Thales, 14, 102
theater, 15–17
    festivals and, 90
    Theater of Dionysus, 15–16, 17
Theocritus, 120
Theophrastus, 118, 119, 123
Thesmophoriazusae (Aristophanes),
    79–81
Thrace, 27
Thucydides, 102
Timaeus (Plato), 15
Titans, 62, 66–68
trade, 88–89
    grain shipping and, 86–87

Uranus (deity), 61–63, 65–66

Venus of Milo (sculpture), 121

Wardman, A.E., 28
wars
    capture of slaves in, 27
    role of slaves in, 29
    see also Peloponnesian War
Wheelwright, Philip, 125
wine, 52
women, 10, 16, 23
    Athenian compared to Spartan,
        18–19
    in comedy by Aristophanes,
        79–81
    education of, 20–21, 24
    limited rights of, 17
    new view of, reflected in art,
        123–24
    separation of, from males, 47,
        48, 72
    as slaves, 27
    wifely role of, described by
        Xenophon, 35, 38–41
    as taught by husband, 36–37

Xenophon, 15, 35, 49, 55

Zeus, 64–67, 109
    Games at Nemea held in honor
        of, 94
    Olympic Games held in honor
        of, 92–93, 95

About the Editor

Historian Don Nardo has written or edited numerous volumes about the ancient Greek world, including *Greek and Roman Sport, The Age of Pericles, The Parthenon, Life in Ancient Athens, The Decline and Fall of Ancient Greece*, and literary companions to the works of Homer, Euripides, and Sophocles. He resides with his wife Christine in Massachusetts.